THE ORIGINS OF
AMERICAN
SLAVERY

ALSO BY BETTY WOOD

Slavery in Colonial Georgia, 1730–1776

*Women's Work, Men's Work: The Informal Slave
Economies of Lowcountry Georgia, 1750–1830*

THE ORIGINS OF
AMERICAN
SLAVERY

*Freedom and Bondage in
the English Colonies*

BETTY WOOD

A CRITICAL ISSUE
CONSULTING EDITOR: ERIC FONER

 HILL AND WANG

A division of Farrar, Straus and Giroux

New York

Hill and Wang
A division of Farrar, Straus and Giroux
19 Union Square West, New York 10003

Distributed in Canada by Douglas & McIntyre Ltd.
Printed in the United States of America
Designed by Jonathan D. Lippincott
First published in 1997 by Hill and Wang
First paperback edition, 1998
7 9 11 10 8
The Library of Congress has catalogued the hardcover edition as follows:
Wood, Betty.
    The origins of American slavery : freedom and bondage in the
English colonies / Betty Wood. — 1st ed.
        p.   cm. — (A Critical issue)
    Includes bibliographical references and index.
    ISBN 0-8090-7456-7 (hardcover : alk. paper)
    1. Slavery—United States—History—17th century.   2. United
States—History—Colonial period, ca. 1600–1775.   I. Title.
II. Series.
E446.W87   1997
973.2—DC20   96-36025

For Lorna, Lynda, and Suzanne,
with love

Contents

THE ORIGINS OF
AMERICAN
SLAVERY

EASTERN
NORTH AMERICA
IN 1700

NEWFOUNDLAND

QUEBEC

L. Superior

L. Huron

L. Michigan

L. Ontario

N.H.

N.Y.

MASS.

R.I.

CONN

ATLANTIC

OCEAN

L. Erie

PA

N J

Mississippi R.

MD

DEL

VIRGINIA

BERMUDA

CAROLINA

FLORIDA

GULF OF

MEXICO

BAHAMAS

PUERTO
RICO

CUBA

HISPANIOLA

JAMAICA

0   Miles   500

THE ANTILLES
AND THE
SPANISH MAIN

1700

0   100   200   300   400   500 Miles

ATLANTIC

OCEAN

PUERTO
RICO

HISPANIOLA

ST EUSTATIUS

ST. CHRISTOPHER
(ST KITTS)

NEVIS

ANTIGUA

CARIBBEAN

SEA

LESSER

ANTILLES

ST LUCIA

BARBADOS

THE GRENADINES

TOBAGO

TORTUGA

TRINIDAD

NEW GRANADA

GUIANA

VICEROYALTY

OF

BRAZIL

Introduction

"The tawny Moore, blacke Negro, duskie Libyan, ash-coloured Indian, [and the] olive coloured American," wrote the Reverend Samuel Purchas in 1614, should be one "sheepfold" with the English and other Europeans, "without any more distinction of Colour, Nation, Language, Sex, [or] Condition." Nowhere in seventeenth-century English America would the equality dreamed of by Purchas be realized.

Toward the close of the seventeenth century, in 1680, another clergyman, Morgan Godwyn, painted a very different picture of the harsh reality that had come to characterize each of the colonies planted by the English in the New World. Godwyn, who had worked in Barbados as an Anglican missionary, observed that in English America, "these two words, *Negro* and *Slave* [are] by custom grown Homogeneous and Convertible; even as *Negro* and *Christian*, *Englishman* and *Heathen*, are by the like Custom and Partiality made Opposites."

Although Godwyn omitted to mention that there were small numbers of "free" people of African descent in each of the English American colonies, and that in parts of the North American mainland the English had enslaved, and would continue to enslave, indigenous Americans, his observation was essentially correct. By 1680, in colonies as different as Massachusetts and Barbados, the widespread assumption of English colonists, and the universal reality of life for an ever-increasing number of Africans, was that to be a Negro meant to be a slave, and vice versa.

Morgan Godwyn's comment raises two critically important questions that have long vexed historians of seventeenth-century English America. Why did the English colonists and their English sponsors, as well as English churchmen and successive English governments, feel able to enslave people of West African descent? What prompted them to do it?

Whatever the other points of difference in their explanations and interpretations, scholars are in complete agreement on one crucial issue: the English did not embark on their colonization of the New World in the late sixteenth century with the explicit intention of enslaving anyone. Why was it, then, that a legal status completely unknown in the Common Law of England was recognized in Barbados as early as 1636 and in Massachusetts by 1641? Why was it that by the middle years of the seventeenth century, everywhere in English America the status of slave, with all that it entailed, became reserved for those of West African ancestry rather than for native Americans or for certain Europeans? What was it about West Africans that made them seem to the English to be suitable, and even ideal, candidates for enslavement? What was it that saved Europeans, including some English people, and most indigenous Americans from this particular fate? The answers to these questions are to be found in an extremely complicated and, as far as students of early English America are concerned, a highly controversial blend of economic, social, religious, and ethnic imperatives.

Over the years historians have favored one of two explanations for the enslavement of West African peoples. Some see it as a process emerging out of a racial ideology that, even before the English began to colonize the New World, had identified West Africans as potential candidates for enslavement. Others downplay the initial significance of ethnicity and claim that economic and demographic considerations largely explain the substitution of involuntary African workers for indentured European servants in the English plantation colonies.

In this interpretation, the English acted in a pragmatic, economically rational manner. Economic necessity and a quest for profits drove them to enslave West Africans. Those who favor this line of argument emphasize that in each of the English plantation colonies, with the exception of South Carolina, the initial legal status of West Africans was ambiguous. Those who had been taken against their will to early Virginia and Barbados may have been regarded by the English as being different from themselves, and were discriminated against on the basis of their ethnicity, but they were not immediately consigned to the legal status of slave. That status, the argument continues, followed in the wake of economic and social practice. The racist theory that underpinned the slave laws that began to be drawn up during the second half of the seventeenth century was a post hoc phenomenon.

The economic argument must loom large in any attempt to explain the precise timing of the transition from indentured to involuntary servitude. Economic considerations alone, however, do not satisfactorily explain why slavery became a status reserved principally for people of West African ancestry. Albeit with the benefit of hindsight, it would seem that from the outset American slavery was characterized by an awareness of ethnic difference that over the course of a century hardened into an overt racism, a racial contempt and hatred that was deliberately cultivated by those who stood to gain financially from the employment of enslaved Africans. Certainly there is evidence of racial prejudice in sixteenth- and early-seventeenth-century England. That prejudice alone, however, did not account for the enslavement of West Africans by the English in the New World. A preexisting English racial awareness would make possible, but did not of itself dictate, the enslavement of West Africans in the Americas.

The different slave systems that emerged in seventeenth-century English America were not the products of either racial prejudice or economic ambition alone, but reflected the complex interaction of both these themes. That a certain level of racial awareness, rooted in English perceptions of themselves and of those they regarded as "outsiders" and "strangers," facilitated the enslavement of West Africans is indisputable. But it was also the case that the adoption of slavery, principally for economic reasons, served only to further harden racial attitudes. The economic imperatives of planters, which became increasingly linked with their political and social aspirations, ensured that race would become an increasingly important, and an increasingly unambiguous, issue.

By the end of the seventeenth century the outcome of quite considered decisions taken by eminent planters in the southern mainland and the English Caribbean was not simply slaveholding societies but slave societies. What differentiated them from the slaveholding colonies of New England and the Middle Atlantic was the extent to which an ideology of racial difference was fast becoming deeply entrenched. Racial slavery had become a central and, from the elite perspective, an absolutely indispensable institution. By 1700 there was no longer any uncertainty, let alone any serious misgivings, about the status of Africans anywhere in English America.

1

Freedom and Bondage in English Thought

The adoption of chattel slavery by the English in their New World colonies had no clear precedent in either English law or social and economic practice. Unlike Spain and Portugal, who by the late fifteenth century were already enslaving West Africans in their domestic economies, the English had no prior model of slavery to serve them in the Americas. What they did have, though, were well-defined concepts of slavery and freedom, of the circumstances under which individuals might be justifiably deprived of their freedom and designated slaves. These concepts were deeply rooted in a knowledge of the slave systems of the ancient world; in biblical, and particularly Old Testament, sources; and in the history of social and economic relationships in England itself.

Bondage was not totally unknown in the English experience, but by the early sixteenth century the medieval practice of serfdom had largely died out. Moreover, in the English definition and practice of this form of servitude, the serf had never been a slave but had always retained a raft of legal and personal rights. To the English, the word *slave* meant a piece of conveyable property, a chattel, with no legal rights or social status whatsoever. In every sense, the slave was deemed to be an outsider. The serf, on the other hand, had the guarantee of limited freedoms and rights. For the slave the loss of freedom and rights was total, perpetual, and usually hereditary. Under certain circumstances the slave might be elevated to the status of a servant, but only under the most exceptional of circumstances could a servant be demoted to the status of a slave.

A central and persistent theme in the abstract English concept of slavery was the notion that the loss of liberty entailed in enslavement was tantamount to the loss of humanity; that the slave was no longer a person, a man or a woman, but an animal. By the sixteenth century, in keeping with other Western Europeans, the English had fairly clear, and long-standing, views about the circumstances under which such a total denial of humanity could be justified. By the same token, they had also satisfied themselves as to the attributes that protected the individual against the complete dehumanization of enslavement.

Ethnicity per se did not loom large in sixteenth-century English discourses on slavery and freedom, and it was not offered by elite English commentators, including those who by the middle of the century were beginning to advocate the colonization of the New World, as either a reason or a sufficient justification for enslavement. The English justification of enslavement was framed in precisely the same terms as prevalent continental European assumptions about the origins of slavery, and initially those assumptions were grounded in religious rather than in ethnic differences.

The beginnings of slavery, European thinkers had long held, as well as an unimpeachable justification for that institution, could be found in the Book of Genesis. Shortly after the Flood, Noah's son Ham sinned by looking upon his father's nakedness. Noah decreed that as a punishment Ham's son Canaan (and by implication his descendants) would forever be "a servant of servants." Based on this biblical source, European thinkers forged a close association between slavery and sin.

A second major theme in European thinking about slavery, which took on a profoundly religious dimension during the Middle Ages, had to do with the relationship between slavery and captivity. Most Europeans believed that individuals captured in a just war had forfeited not only their freedom but also their very lives to their captors. The latter enjoyed the right to do as they would with such captives: they could put them to the sword or, if they preferred, they might legitimately enslave them. In the Christian tradition, of course, crusades and just wars were waged not against other Christians but against infidels, against heathens, against outsiders.

By the sixteenth century the link between the lack of Christianity and the eligibility for enslavement had long been in place. What was to prove problematical for the English, in the Old World and in the New, were other aspects of the relationship between Christianity and slavery. Could one Christian legitimately hold another Christian as a slave? Did conversion to Christianity comprise an irrefutable case for manumission (freeing of the enslaved person)? What were the duties and obligations of Christian masters and mistresses toward those they held as slaves? As we shall see, the essentially self-serving answers to these questions arrived at by the English were to be critically important in fundamentally reshaping the basis upon which the status of individuals, and groups of individuals, would be determined in their American colonies.

If sixteenth-century English people had an albeit abstract concept of slavery, of the circumstances under which some people might be legitimately and totally deprived of their liberty to the point of being defined as pieces of property, then the same was also true of their definition of those who could expect to escape such a fate. As understood by the English, slavery was a status reserved for strangers, for outsiders, who were defined primarily in terms of their religious preferences rather than by any other characteristic or attribute. It was simply inconceivable to the English elite that they could strip English people of their "rights" and "privileges" and turn them into slaves. If slavery was going to take root in their New World colonies, then it would almost certainly have to involve the enslavement of non-English peoples.

Chattel slavery might have had no place in the thinking of influential proponents of English colonization, but other, traditional forms of English servitude most certainly did. The essentially conservative assumption that underpinned elite English plans for the settlement of the New World was that *English* America would be precisely that. The hierarchical social, economic, religious, and political relationships of England, together with the institutions that sought to sustain them, would be transplanted in their entirety to the Americas. The New World was not envisaged, let alone championed, as a forum in which those relationships and institutions should be, or would be, reinvented. In fact, the very reverse was true.

Beginning in the 1580s with Sir Humphrey Gilbert and Sir Walter Raleigh, and without exception during the course of the next century, those men who were entrusted by the Crown with charters that authorized them to found colonies in the Americas sought to implement their own particular versions of an ideal English society, either past or present, in the New World. The social, economic, and political blueprints they devised were always conservative and sometimes, as was the case with John Winthrop's design for Massachusetts and the Calverts' intentions for Maryland, positively anachronistic.

By the middle years of the sixteenth century the eminent Englishmen who would oversee the organization of societies in the Americas were extolling the glories of English "liberty" and trumpeting the rights and privileges that were enshrined in the Common Law of the land. In this interpretation, English society was nothing if not free and equal. For most English people, however, daily reality was a society characterized by a strong sense of hierarchy. The Great Chain of Being provided theoretical support for the proposition that social rank was predetermined and unalterable, that some were born to be gentlemen and to govern while others, the majority, were fated to be poor and to provide labor, and this was the actuality of life in sixteenth- and early-seventeenth-century England.

An array of institutional devices sought to ensure the persistence of the elite ideal of an ordered and orderly society. In many aspects of their daily lives ordinary people were being constantly reminded of the lowly place they occupied in this rigidly stratified and immutable social order. Differentiations of wealth and of social status were readily apparent in the clothing people wore, in the houses they lived in, in the food they ate, and in where they sat in church on Sundays. Those who filled the lower ranks of this hierarchical social order were expected to know and keep to their place. If they did not, their self-styled superiors were quick to act to restore the social order.

Sixteenth-century governments, both central and local, sanctioned the strict and harsh control of the lower orders, of beggars and vagrants, of anyone whose behavior seemed to be challenging the accepted order and ordering of society. Those in the lower reaches of sixteenth-century English society might lay claim to the liberties, privileges, and rights of Englishmen, and take enormous pride in their "Englishness," but while they remained in England they stood virtually no chance of partaking of the freedom enjoyed by those who occupied the upper ranks of their society.

Dependency or the lack of it was central to the sixteenth-century English concept of freedom and to the political rights associated with that freedom. Those who were dependent on others for their livelihood, those who had no direct, landed stake in society, were disqualified from full and equal partici- pation in political society. Such a definition embraced the vast majority of the English population in the sixteenth and seven- teenth centuries and, in a great many cases, did so in a way that was to have profound implications for the English colo- nization of the Americas.

Servitude of one sort or another, and therefore dependency, was a widespread practice in England. The relationship be- tween servant and employer usually involved a contractual ar- rangement, which might be verbal or written. Contracts were normally drawn up annually, but sometimes they could involve a longer term of employment. Servants might be regarded as being dependent, but they were dependents who retained crit- ically important legal rights with respect to their labor and their persons.

That this labor system might be extended to the New World was suggested as early as 1583 by Sir George Peckham, and its basic elements were evident in the plans drawn up by the Vir- ginia Company for its colony. What came to be known as in- dentured servitude was an extension of English theory and practice to the New World. In terms of the numbers involved, the system of indentured servitude was to prove remarkably successful. Seventy-five to 80 percent of all the people who left England for the Chesapeake during the seventeenth century went as indentured servants. The transportation of indentured servants, principally to the plantation colonies of the southern mainland and the West Indies, rapidly developed into what has been described as one of the big businesses of the seventeenth century.

The seventeenth-century elite English view of indentured servants was, to say the least, unflattering. They were described by one writer as "idle, lazy, simple people such as have professed idleness and will rather beg than work." In the middle years of the century one English visitor to Barbados commented, "Rogues and whores and such like people are those which are generally brought here." Barbados, he concluded, was "the dunghill whereon England doth cast forth its rubbish." These comments reveal rather more about those who made them than they do about the character and morality of indentured servants. Elite English commentators were horrified, and frightened, by the mobility associated with indentured servitude. The men and women who roamed around England during hard economic times in search of work, and who sometimes ended up on ships bound for the Americas, presented what to elite English people was the fearful specter of social disorder. One of the ways in which they could comfort themselves was by suggesting that these migrants were rogues, whores, and vagabonds, people of little social and economic worth, and even less morality, whose departure from England was no bad thing.

In recent years there has been some dispute as to the actual social origins, and prior occupational experience, of those who crossed to the plantation colonies as indentured servants. It appears that over half of those who made their way to the Chesapeake colonies, and whose occupation was recorded, came from agricultural backgrounds. Around one-fifth of the remainder were semiskilled or skilled workers, drawn mainly from the textile and clothing trades.

The age and sex of indentured servants is far less difficult to determine. Most were between their mid-teens and mid-twenties; men outnumbered women by as many as five or six to one; and the vast majority of servants were unmarried at the time they left England. When combined with the hazardous epidemiological environments encountered in early Virginia and Barbados, this imbalanced sex ratio was to militate against family formation and the natural increase of population. There were to be many social and economic consequences stemming from this inability of the early settlers to reproduce themselves, but one of the most important of them was the failure to produce a workforce of a sufficient size to satisfy future labor requirements.

Some scholars have identified the antecedents of chattel slavery in indentured servitude, and there is certainly more than a grain of truth in such a view. For different lengths of time in each of England's plantation colonies, indentured servants provided the large, fixed workforces considered necessary for the intensive cultivation of crops such as tobacco and sugar. From the outset an element of dependency, unfreedom, and coercion was built into the economic, and thereby the political, arrangements devised by the English for the material exploitation of their American colonies. There were to be several important differences, however, between the indentured servitude of Europeans and the involuntary servitude of West Africans.

Indenture entailed service for a limited, predetermined number of years. In practice children might follow the same occupation as one or the other of their parents, but in a strictly legal sense the status of an indentured servant was not inherited. The terms and conditions of indentured servitude were usually set out in a legally binding contract. That contract might be sold, bartered, given away, or even gambled away by the master or mistress, but what was being disposed of was the servant's labor and not the servant's person. Finally, the legal and personal rights of indentured servants were never subject to the same process of erosion that came to characterize the slave systems of English America. In many respects it would be the legally binding guarantee of eventual freedom that differentiated indentured servitude from chattel slavery.

Colonial proprietors and employers may have wished to continue with the employment practices of the Old World in the New, but those practices, especially in the plantation colonies, had to be modified in a profoundly significant way in order to persuade a sufficient number of workers to cross the Atlantic. English men and women, even those from the most humble social backgrounds, had to be offered some incentive to move to the New World. At the very least they had to be offered more, either in material or in nonmaterial terms, than they could expect to achieve by remaining in England. The bait that was held out to them was something that was virtually denied to them in England, something they might aspire to but could not realistically hope to acquire if they remained in the Old World. That something was land, and the freedom that went with it. As Captain John Smith put it in 1614, in America "Every man may be master of his own labour and land; or the greatest portion in a small time."

At the very least, land ownership offered the possibility of wealth, potentially enormous wealth. It also offered prestige, respectability, and admission into political society. For pragmatic rather than idealistic reasons, elite English colonizers were forced to concede that membership in political society would be the eventual reward for all those of their male compatriots, however lowly their English origins, willing to cross to America as indentured servants. The freedom on offer to prospective migrants was neither immediate nor unconditional, but it was no less attractive for that.

Those willing to indenture themselves for a term of years, usually five, in exchange for their passage to America and their maintenance while they remained under contract, proved reluctant to forfeit their freedom and reenter the labor market as servants at the end of their indenture. This fact was to have significant implications for the maintenance of the large workforces deemed necessary for plantation agriculture. If those workforces could not be maintained by natural increase, by the reemployment of former servants, or by a continuing flow of indentured servants from the Old World, then alternative sources of labor would have to be sought.

By the 1620s and 1630s three groups were already being contemplated as prospective workers: other Europeans, indigenous Americans, and West Africans. The question that remained, and would be determined at different times in the different colonies, was which of these groups most appropriately fitted the labor requirements of the English. It also remained to be seen precisely what status would be accorded to any members of these groups who could be persuaded, or coerced, into working for the English and how long they would be expected to retain that status.

For those colonists who knew or cared about them, the elite discourses of sixteenth-century England defined Englishness in a way that suggested that freedom as understood by the English would not be readily extended to indigenous Americans or to other "foreigners" in the New World. Those same discourses, as well as English practice, also served to sanction unfreedom in the form of a servile status and in certain circumstances allowed for the enslavement of outsiders. What in sixteenth-century English thought was the theoretical possibility of enslavement would be converted into social and economic reality by the colonists of seventeenth-century English America. For essentially practical reasons, they would find chattel slavery both a viable and a perfectly acceptable means of providing the assured and permanent workforces they considered necessary for the maintenance of their own freedom.

As we shall now go on to see, the images of West Africa and its inhabitants that formed in sixteenth-century England, as well as the colonial practices of England's European rivals in the New World, raised the distinct possibility that the vast majority of those selected to fill this role would be people of West African descent. There were, however, others who were equally vulnerable to exploitation by the English in the New World. Such was the nature and the intensity of sixteenth-century English ethnocentricity that, should the need ever arise, native Americans too could be made to conform to the abstract English concept of slavery. But it is important to bear in mind that, as the English stood poised to begin their colonization of the Americas, neither enslavement nor the enslavement of West Africans was by any means a foregone conclusion.

2

"Beastly Lyvynge": Images of West Africans and Native Americans

The enslavement of West Africans by the English in their New World colonies was a seventeenth-century phenomenon, but the roots of that enslavement lay in racial attitudes that took shape during the course of the previous century. There is some suggestion that, even before they embarked on their colonization of the North American mainland and the Caribbean, the English were already predisposed to regard West Africans as suitable candidates for enslavement. This did not necessarily mean that they would enslave Africans, but it did mean the colonists were likely to turn to Africans to satisfy their labor requirements.

Sixteenth-century English people regarded themselves, their nation, as the very personification of civilization; they were at the hub. The outer rings of the wheel of civilization were represented, in order of their divergence from the English model, by the Welsh and the Scots, the continental European Protestants, the Irish Roman Catholics, and the continental European Roman Catholics. These peoples were judged against English standards and, without exception, found deficient. The attempt to introduce, and if necessary to impose, the English ideal of civilization informed England's dealings with the nations and peoples they encountered close to home during the course of the sixteenth century: the Scots, the Welsh, and, with enormous consequences for their ventures in the New World, the Irish. Two peoples whom the English encountered for the first time in the sixteenth century, native Americans and West Africans, were placed at the extreme limits, and by some beyond the pale, of civilization as defined and understood by the English.

It is important, however, that we do not impose seventeenth-century imperatives and interpretations on sixteenth-century English people. The images of West Africa that developed in sixteenth-century England were far from flattering, and at a comparatively early date the association was being made between West Africans and chattel slavery. Yet those in high places who advocated the overseas expansion of England did not propose that West Africans could, should, or would be enslaved by the English in the Americas. Indeed, West Africans scarcely figured at all in the sixteenth-century English agenda for the New World. When they did, it was usually in the context of their enslavement by two of England's main European rivals, Spain and Portugal.

Those who perforce loomed large in English thinking about, and plans for, the New World were the indigenous populations of the Americas. In many respects, sixteenth-century English images of native Americans were not entirely dissimilar to those they were simultaneously constructing of West Africans. Both were strangers, both were apparently uncivilized, and both were dark-skinned. The English used native Americans and West Africans alike as "social mirrors." That is to say, they set both groups against themselves to emphasize what they conceived of as being completely different qualities of religious, social, and political organization, sexual behavior, and skin color.

Sometimes native Americans and West Africans were fused together in the popular imagination. In 1588, for example, in Marlowe's play *Dr. Faustus*, native Americans were referred to as "Indian Moors." For this reason, it is clear that the enslavement of Africans must have come about for other, practical reasons, not just those of attitude or impression. The fact remains, however, that there *were* English impressions of West Africans that raised the possibility that they might be legitimate candidates for enslavement. These impressions had antecedents that long predated the first direct encounters between the English and West Africans in the sixteenth century. Over the years, elite Englishmen had formed some of their impressions of Africa and its inhabitants through their reading of the works of ancient Greek and Roman writers. For more humble English men and women, the Bible was an important, and before the sixteenth century probably the main, source of information about Africa and African peoples. By the late fifteenth century, however, the English were beginning to receive other, nonliterary accounts that would be influential in shaping their racial ideology. They learned, for example, that Spain and Portugal were not only employing West Africans but enslaving them in their domestic economies. By the early sixteenth century the English also knew that the Iberian powers were doing the same in their New World colonies.

It was not until 1530 that the English began to acquire a firsthand knowledge of West Africa. In that year William Hawkins, of Plymouth, made the first recorded English voyage to West Africa. Unlike his son John some thirty years later, William Hawkins went to Africa to trade with, rather than in, West Africans. He did not leave a detailed account of his impressions of those he did business with, but later travelers and traders published accounts of their experiences that were to be of enormous significance in shaping English perceptions of West Africa and its inhabitants. It is virtually impossible to document the stories and tales that ordinary sailors who had voyaged to the West Coast of Africa told their families and friends upon their return to England. But they must have played a part in defining the attitudes of the nonelite, and often illiterate, people from among whom many of the early American colonists would subsequently be recruited.

The published accounts of West Africa and its peoples that appeared in sixteenth-century England drew attention to several points of difference between West Africans and the English. More than anything else it was the blackness of West Africans that at once fascinated and repelled English commentators. The negative connotations that the English had long attached to the color black were to deeply prejudice their assessment of West Africans. If, as the English believed, the color black epitomized sin and evil, then presumably those same defects must attach to the black-skinned person.

The blackness of West Africans also posed another problem for the English. Christian theology suggested that all humanity originated from a single source, from Adam and Eve, who were assumed by European thinkers to have been fair-skinned, so how was the blackness of Africans to be explained? If it could not be satisfactorily explained, did this mean that West Africans were not part of the common creation, that they were not human? English attempts to account for the West African's blackness included climatic explanations that lost their force when those who were taken to the colder climes of Northern Europe retained their skin color and gave birth to black children. Other explanations included quasi-genetic assumptions about West

Africans and, of crucial significance, the argument that they were the descendants of Ham. (Ham sinned against his father, Noah, and as punishment Noah cursed Ham's son, Canaan, to a life of slavery.) The English could therefore conclude that slavery had originated as a divine punishment for sinful behavior.

If the blackness of West Africans had made a deep and disturbing impact on the English, then so did their religion, or, more specifically, what the English regarded as their lack of it. What English observers depicted as the superstitious, magical beliefs and practices of West Africans, and their apparent unwillingness to embrace Christianity, marked them out in the English mind as not only different but also decidedly inferior. Eventually the English, like other Europeans, would cite the heathenism of West Africans as one of the justifications for their enslavement.

A third English impression had to do with the social structures and practices they encountered in West Africa. English visitors found little, if anything, with which they could identify. On the contrary, they were shocked and appalled by social arrangements and behavior that seemed to them to be the very antithesis of civilized English society. Marriage and family arrangements, for example, were measured against English yardsticks and deemed to be indicative of the West African's irremediable savagery. If any one comment encapsulated English views about the deficiencies of West African societies compared with their own, then it was Richard Eden's observation of the mid-1550s, republished by Richard Hakluyt in 1589, that those "which we now call Moores, Moorens, or Negroes, [are] a people of beastly lyvynge, without a god, law, religion, or common wealth."

Other English writers reiterated Eden's allusions to the

"beastly lyvynge" of West Africans. They regaled their readers not with descriptions of West Africans as innocent, noble savages who might be elevated to some degree of civility by Europeans, but as wild, barbarous people who bore more than a passing similarity to animals. Indeed, when describing the physical characteristics of West Africans, some English commentators made direct comparisons between them and animals. It was to be no coincidence that such comparisons often involved the anthropoid ape, the animal that most closely resembled man and that sixteenth-century English visitors to West Africa were being introduced to for the first time. One fairly typical example of the comments that were made by the English was the observation that West African "men that have low and flat nostrils are libidinous as apes that attempt women." Another author, one of several who were appalled by the nakedness of many West Africans, especially the women, remarked that "the men and women go so alike, that one cannot know a man from a woman but by their breasts, which in the most part be very foule and long, hanging downe low like the udder of a goate." Such accounts called into serious question the very humanity of West Africans.

Images that were formed as the English and West Africans encountered one another in Africa were profoundly important in shaping English attitudes. From the mid-1550s onward, however, what would prove to be permanent encounters between the English and West Africans would take place in a very different context: in England itself. Ordinary English people would no longer have to rely on secondhand reports produced by commentators working out their own agendas: they could see and assess West Africans for themselves.

The first English voyages to West Africa had been made with a view to exploiting material, rather than human, wealth, and this also was the intention of John Lok, who set sail for Africa in 1554. The following year he returned to England, bringing back with him five West African men. It seems that these men were the first West Africans to set foot in England, and their arrival marked the beginnings of a black British population. The men in question had come to England willingly. Lok's sole motive was to facilitate English trading links with West Africa. He intended that these five men should be taught English, and something about English commercial practices, and then returned home to act as intermediaries between the English and their prospective West African trading partners.

During the next few decades a growing number of West Africans, women as well as men, followed in the footsteps of the first five. But there was a critically important difference: those who arrived in England during the latter part of the sixteenth century were taken there against their will. Their arrival was an incidental result of the apparently uncritical enthusiasm with which some Englishmen sought to enter the growing transatlantic slave trade.

By the early 1560s there were those in England who, driven by the prospect of profits and displaying no moral qualms, sought to exploit the opportunities offered by the enslavement of West Africans in the Iberian New World colonies. The beginnings of what by the late seventeenth century would become a highly profitable transatlantic slave trade for the English, and for some of the American colonists also, can be traced to 1562, when John Hawkins left England for West Africa. Unlike his father, that first English trader to West Africa, John Hawkins went there to secure not material goods but labor. He sailed "to the coast of Guinea . . . where he stayed some time and got into his possession, partly by the sword and partly by other means," around 300 Africans, whom he was able to sell at a profit to the labor-hungry Spanish settlers in Hispaniola. Largely because of the deteriorating relations between England and Spain over the next few years, which in the late sixteenth century culminated in all-out war, and partly because of Spanish resistance to foreign interlopers in any branch of their highly lucrative colonial trade, Hawkins's subsequent slaving ventures were far less successful.

Other traders sought to emulate Hawkins, and it was through them that many West Africans were brought to England. Sometimes the captains of slave ships transported Africans at their own expense, and disposed of them in England as well as in the Americas. Similarly, captains engaged in other forms of trade with West Africa might have brought Africans to England. In either event, by the end of the sixteenth century there was a significant black presence in England, mainly in London and the country's other major port towns. The people who lived in these towns, or who passed through them on their way to the Americas, were in a position to form their own images and impressions of West Africans.

Comparatively little is known about the size, distribution, and precise legal status of England's black population as of about 1700. English law provided no clear precedents when it came to determining the legal status of these West African newcomers and their children. As it stood, the Common Law did not entertain the possibility of chattel slavery in England. But did this mean that chattel slavery could never exist in the land? Could those people of West African descent who were born in England legitimately claim all the liberties and rights of freeborn Englishmen? These questions would vex the English legal establishment for the next century and a half, the more so once the American colonists had legitimated chattel slavery in their societies. Would the property rights the colonists claimed in their slaves remain valid if they brought those slaves to England for any reason? Over the years English jurists and courts took conflicting positions on the issue.

The precise legal status of England's black population in the late sixteenth century is open to question, but there is no evidence of any parliamentary legislation or judicial decisions that stated categorically that they were chattels. Rather more can be said about blacks' social and economic status. All the evidence indicates that they were consigned to lowly, servile occupations. For some this might mean employment as the personal servant of an eminent individual who gained even more prestige by being able to flaunt a black attendant. For many, probably most, West Africans, life in England entailed menial occupations that brought them into frequent contact with the lower-class English people who performed similar kinds of work themselves. Whether there was intense competition between nonelite English and African workers or whether relations between them were cordial, with their shared lowly rank assuming a greater importance in their lives than their ethnic differences, must remain a matter for conjecture. (Once these groups reached America, though, there is some evidence that they forged mutually supportive relationships.)

Thus, by the end of the sixteenth century English impressions of West Africans were based on the literary and verbal reports of those who had visited West Africa and, increasingly, on an African presence in England itself. Attitudes were also affected by the Iberian model; for many decades the English had known that, both in Europe and in the Americas, West Africans had been selected as suitable candidates for enslavement by the Spanish and the Portuguese. But even knowledge of the Iberian example by no means dictated that the English would enslave West Africans in their own colonies. Indeed, there were those English who saw those West Africans already in the New World as prospective allies in their ongoing struggle against Spain.

It is only with the benefit of hindsight that one can say that the highly negative images and impressions of West Africans formed by the English during the sixteenth century made them vulnerable to enslavement in seventeenth-century English America. But if West Africans were possible candidates for enslavement by the English, could not the same be said of those who could not be easily ignored by English colonizers, those who had to figure prominently in their plans for the New World: the indigenous peoples of the Americas? On the face of it, some of the attributes ascribed to them by English commentators would seem to have made them just as exposed as West Africans to the possibility of enslavement.

In marked contrast to the unanimity among scholars concerning the negative English attitudes toward West Africans, historians have been sharply divided in their assessments of the impressions that the English were simultaneously forming of the indigenous peoples of the Americas. On the one hand, there are those who argue that there was comparatively little difference in English perceptions of the two groups. In this interpretation, both peoples were held to be inferior to the English; both peoples were despised by the English on account of their heathenism, their skin color, and their reputed lack of civility; and, at one time or another, both peoples, and not just West Africans, had their humanity called into question by the English. Native Americans therefore slotted just as neatly into the sixteenth-century English concept of who might be eligible for enslavement as did West Africans.

On the other side are those scholars who insist that, not always for the most innocent or altruistic of reasons, the English quickly developed a far more positive impression of native Americans than they ever would of West Africans. Central to this scholarly scenario is the claim that the English who encountered native Americans, and those who remained in England to write about them in a more detached fashion, found much with which they could identify, and much to admire, in the indigenous peoples and cultures of the New World. Like West Africans, this line of argument continues, native Americans were assessed against the yardstick of English civilization and found wanting, but, unlike West Africans, they were not regarded as morally and culturally irredeemable. English commentators detected, perhaps because for pragmatic reasons they wished to detect them, qualities and attributes that would make it possible for indigenous Americans to acquire at least the veneer of English civilization. Here were simple, innocent people, noble savages, who remained "ignorant" only because they had never been exposed to the blessings and benefits of English culture. Not only were they intellectually capable of absorbing the imperatives of that culture, and particularly of the Christian theology that informed so much of it, but they were willing, eager even, to be "civilized" by the English. These were people with whom the English felt that they could coexist in perfect harmony.

The truth of the matter is that from the outset both these strands were found in the English imaging of native Americans. This contrasted sharply with the universally negative English stereotyping of West Africans, but, even so, these conflicting perceptions of native Americans by no means ruled out the possibility of their eventual enslavement. Indeed, by the 1570s and 1580s, as English plans for colonizing the New World were fast taking shape, the negative aspects of their stereotyping of indigenous Americans were coming increasingly to the fore.

Unlike their compatriots who set out to develop trading links with West Africa, the first English voyagers to the New World were not encumbered with long-standing myths and legends about who and what they would find there. Of course, this is not to say that they crossed the Atlantic Ocean with a completely open mind. On the contrary, they took with them precisely the same social and cultural imperatives that were simultaneously helping to inform English perceptions of West African peoples. Commentators would either find what they sought in the New World or choose to interpret what they found in ways that conformed to their intentions for the Americas.

Like their European rivals, particularly the Spanish, the English were attracted to the New World principally by the wealth it offered: by the fish and furs that formed the basis of the initial trading links they forged with the indigenous peoples of Newfoundland and the eastern seaboard of the North American mainland; and by the prospect of finding a northwest passage that would enable them to bypass their European rivals (who were operating in the Indian Ocean) and use a shorter, safer route to the riches of the Orient. Last, but by no means least, the English were lured across the Atlantic by the precious metals that were then flowing back to Spain in such abundance that they seemed likely to fundamentally reshape the balance of power in the Old World. The English wished to share in that wealth and, once they had made the break with Rome in the mid-sixteenth century, to halt the march of Roman Catholicism across both the Old World and the New.

From the beginning native Americans had a clearly defined, and on one level a very pragmatic, role to play in England's blueprint for the New World. Long before they envisaged establishing permanent colonies in the Americas, the English appreciated the enormity of the material benefits that would stem from forging trade links with indigenous Americans. If all went according to plan, the latter would help them to exploit the raw materials that America had to offer and would simultaneously provide an immense new market for English manufactures. If the English plan succeeded, the material cultures of their native American trading partners would be changed, and from the English perspective changed only for the better, by virtue of this economic association.

The English soon began to carve out two other interrelated roles for indigenous Americans: not only would the natives be important economic partners in the struggle that England was waging with Spain, they could also serve as invaluable military and religious allies. Their conversion to Christianity, to Protestant Christianity, was seen by many in England, by non-churchmen as well as by the Anglican clergy, as one way of stemming the further spread of Roman Catholicism in the New World. Protestantism would cross the Atlantic with the English, and native Americans would be the primary vehicles for its subsequent expansion throughout the Americas. All these interlocking imperatives played a part in shaping, and would in their turn be shaped by, English perceptions of the indigenous populations of the New World.

Although some commentators made reference to the savagery of native Americans in a language comparable to that simultaneously being employed by English travelers to describe West Africans, the initial impressions formed by the English of the peoples they were encountering in North America were generally favorable. Those who crossed the Atlantic in search of fish and furs freely acknowledged the assistance they received from indigenous Americans. They admitted that the fur trade, upon which the English pinned such high economic hopes, depended upon the superior tracking and hunting skills of their native American associates. True, these people who were so adept at exploiting their natural environments differed from themselves in their physical appearance, and particularly in their skin color; but they were not so strikingly different from themselves as were West African peoples. In the New World there was no blackness, with all that this entailed for the evolving relationship between West Africans and Europeans, for the English to explain.

What English and other European thinkers did find it necessary to explain, though, was the entirely unanticipated presence of people in a part of the world hitherto unknown to them. How had they got there? Where had they come from and when? As with their discourses on the blackness of West Africans, Europeans felt that they must find a way of reconciling the existence of an American populace with the Christian belief in a common creation. The theological solution they arrived at was very different from, and far more flattering to native Americans than, that which they constructed in order to explain the skin color of West Africans.

The indigenous peoples of the New World, some European thinkers believed, were not the accursed offspring of Ham but quite possibly the descendants of one of the lost tribes of Israel. According to this line of reasoning native Americans were, in effect, a people of distant European ancestry, a people who, through no real fault of their own, had missed out on the "civilizing," and particularly the Christianizing, of Western Europe. Unlike the inhabitants of West Africa, the native populations of the New World could be depicted as possessing what Saint Paul believed to be the natural godliness of some heathens who had not been exposed to Christian teaching.

In part because it suited their purposes in being in America to do so, the English detected what might be described as various "European" qualities and attributes in native Americans and their cultures, qualities and attributes with which they could readily identify. Although slightly darker than their own, the skin color of native Americans, together with the texture of their hair and their facial features, could be interpreted by the English as indicative of their distant European origins. John White's sketches, published in 1590, provide the most vivid visual image of the way in which the physical features of indigenous Americans were "Europeanized" in order to fit English assumptions and requirements.

White's sketches also draw attention to another way in which native Americans were Europeanized by the English. Many writers believed that they could detect in the New World something reminiscent of Europe, and something they thought lacking in West Africa: highly organized societies, nations even, that were characterized by the hierarchy the English so admired. The imposition of English definitions of social status on native Americans, the variations in their clothing and accessories according to their social standing, was there for all to see in John White's portfolio of drawings. His sketches merely confirmed, albeit in a highly significant visual manner, contemporary literary depictions of native Americans as living in highly ordered societies that in the English imagination could be made to bear more than a passing similarity to the elite English ideal of social organization.

The English believed that under their strict supervision the very positive—because they were very European—qualities they detected in the peoples of the New World could be honed and perfected. Moreover, they insisted that it was their responsibility, as well as in their self-interest, to undertake this task. Indigenous Americans, they held, could be guided some

way up, potentially a long way up, the ladder of English civilization. But they could never reach the very top of that ladder, they could never become truly English. The ethnocentricity of the English was such that they were never willing to concede the complete equality of those native Americans who elected to abandon their own cultural heritages and traditions in favor of English civilization.

The arrogant and self-serving English assumption that developed through the middle years of the sixteenth century was not only that native Americans already had many of the qualities necessary for them to attain a significantly higher degree of Europeanization, or more precisely of Anglicization, but that they would positively welcome such a process. If only because they had to be, because their intentions for the New World demanded it, English propagandists were confident that native Americans would conform to the various roles they were in the process of devising for them. But what if they did not? If nothing else, the attempted military subjugation of Ireland by the English, and the reports the English received simultaneously from Spanish America, demonstrated that indigenous peoples did not necessarily see any great merit in adopting the civilization on offer from those who invaded their shores. On the contrary, the projected cultural invasions of Ireland by the English, and of the Americas by the Iberian powers, had met with the most violent resistance. Neither the Spanish in the New World nor, and in the present context more significantly, the English in Ireland had shown any great reluctance to try to impose their will by military means. If the need ever arose, here were important contemporary precedents that the English might well elect to follow in the Americas.

By the 1570s and 1580s English propagandists were well on the way to devising what in effect was a contingency plan that, in their view, could be legitimately implemented should their projected colonization of the Americas encounter armed opposition from the indigenous peoples of the New World. In many ways it was a plan designed to secure for the English the material wealth that they intended to reap from the New World. Obviously, it would be very much to the advantage of the English if they could obtain that wealth without the massive military expenditure that would be entailed in waging all-out war against native Americans. But it became increasingly clear to the English that the potential rewards of the New World were so enormous, potentially so significant for their standing in the Old World, that if it ever became necessary to do so they would resort to whatever physical force, whatever expenditure, was called for in order to secure those rewards.

If only because they had presented such a favorable impression of native Americans, and the ease with which they expected English objectives in the New World to be secured, such eminent proponents of colonization as Sir George Peckham and the two Richard Hakluyts felt the need to provide some theoretical defenses, some justification, of the circumstances under which military force might be employed by the English against the indigenous peoples of the Americas. These commentators sought to emphasize the purity of English intentions toward native Americans: they wished not to dispossess them of the lands to which they had a recognizable moral and legal claim by right of prior occupancy, but only to coexist with them on those lands. The English sought only "just and lawful traffic" with the peoples of the New World. If those peoples should be foolish enough, or ungrateful enough, to reject these peaceable intentions, then the English had every right to defend themselves and their interests. Somewhat optimistically, perhaps, given the likely ratio of English people to indigenous

Americans during the initial years of colonization, Hakluyt the younger confidently asserted that the settlers would be well able to protect themselves and their interests in the New World.

In a language that did not bode well for the future, Sir George Peckham insisted that in the event of the English being attacked by native Americans it would be "no breach of equity for the Christians to defend themselves and to pursue revenge with force." Peckham's implicit reference to the heathenism of indigenous Americans, and the right of Christians to wage just wars against infidels, carried with it the implication that the native populations of the New World could be made to conform to the sixteenth-century English concept of enslavement. For essentially pragmatic reasons English commentators hoped that peaceable relations could be maintained with native Americans, but, at the same time, they felt able to justify the use of military force, for defensive reasons and for revenge, should the need to use such force ever arise.

Native Americans were to receive their first taste of what they might expect from the English soon after the founding of Roanoke in 1587. On the one hand, some of the English settlers wrote glowing reports of the welcome they had received from people who were "most gentle, loving, and faithful, [and] void of all guile and treason," from people who had freely given them a significant amount of material assistance. Such accounts epitomized the positive stereotyping of native Americans and seemed to confirm that they conformed to English expectations of them. The darker side of the English stereotype, however, was also in evidence at Roanoke. When a piece of their property, a silver cup, went missing, the settlers immediately jumped to the conclusion that it must have been taken by native Americans. Some of them reacted with a show of force that others of their number found shocking and excessive. As one settler commented, burning down native American villages and "slaying some of the people" seemed to be "too fierce" a reaction to an incident that "on our part, might easily enough have been borne."

Roanoke provided a highly revealing practical example of the manner in which the English felt able to respond to those native Americans who, in Hakluyt the elder's words, they believed had behaved "injuriously to offend us." The loss of this first English settlement in the New World would serve only to further confirm English suspicions of the "guile," of the duplicity, of native Americans. When in 1591, after a two-year absence, John White returned from England to Roanoke with provisions for the settlement of 117 people, including seventeen women and nine children, the colony had vanished into thin air. Initially White was not too concerned, because he knew that the settlers had intended to move farther inland. He searched for them, but with no success.

From that day to this no one knows for certain what happened to these English people, how and why the colony of Roanoke came to be "lost." But late-sixteenth-century English explanations focused on the part that native Americans might have played in its assumed demise. In the worst-case scenario the English judged them perfectly capable of having slaughtered these English men, women, and children. At the very least, many English believed that the native Americans were guilty of not providing the colonists with much-needed material assistance—an interpretation that was scarcely more flattering.

The short-lived history of Roanoke revealed both sides of the English stereotyping of native Americans, the negative and the positive impressions that had been formed over the better part of a century. Certainly, and if only for self-interested reasons,

English commentators held native Americans in a much higher regard than they ever did West Africans. However, and for equally pragmatic reasons, by the 1570s and 1580s they were also emphasizing that, like West Africans, native Americans were possessed of characteristics and qualities that under certain circumstances could both necessitate and legitimate their brutal repression. Whether that repression would entail their enslavement remained to be seen, but by 1600, when the English were poised to relaunch their attempt to establish a permanent presence in the New World, it was a possibility that could not be entirely ruled out.

3

The First American Slaves: The Caribbean and Carolina

What would ultimately prove to be the permanent English settlement of the New World began at Jamestown in 1607, and the earliest report of a West African presence anywhere in English America dates from Virginia in 1619. In many ways, however, the enslavement of West Africans by the English could be said to have begun not in Virginia but elsewhere in the Americas, in the Caribbean. During the course of the seventeenth century the supply of West African workers to England's mainland plantation colonies, and the treatment they encountered there, would be intimately connected to developments in the English Caribbean. By the mid-1630s the English in Barbados had already devised a slave status for those West Africans already on the island; that would not be true of Virginia until the second half of the seventeenth century.

The activities—the social, economic, and racial imperatives—of those English people who, beginning in the mid-1620s, struggled to secure a foothold in the Caribbean would have a direct and crucial bearing on the course of events in the southern mainland. To suggest otherwise is to impose a false, and what to contemporaries would have been a meaningless, disconnection between these different parts of seventeenth-century English America.

The English first became aware of South America and the Caribbean islands around 1500, and most of what they got to know about these parts of the Americas, their peoples and their physical environments, derived from Spanish and Portuguese reports. It became increasingly clear to the English that if they wished to partake of the riches offered by South America and the West Indian islands, and particularly the precious metals that were adding enormously to Spanish power in the Old World, then there were only two options open to them.

Spain's military might by the 1530s and 1540s, especially in Florida and the western Caribbean islands of Cuba, Hispaniola, and Jamaica, effectively ruled out the possibility of a full-scale frontal attack on the Spanish empire as a whole. But, the English believed, the riches of that empire could be exploited in another way: by launching hit-and-run attacks on the treasure fleets that so regularly traversed the Caribbean on their way back to Spain. Privateering offered those who engaged in it the prospect of securing an enormous return on a comparatively modest capital investment. As Anglo-Spanish relations deteriorated, privateering would assume an aura of respectability, of blows being inflicted by upstanding Protestant Englishmen on their implacable Roman Catholic enemies. What the English needed for logistical reasons more than for anything else were New World bases from which they could launch their privateering enterprises. Dominated as it was by Spain, the western Caribbean offered few prospects for establishing such bases; the eastern Caribbean seemed far more promising.

The English were also well aware that the Iberian powers were extracting another kind of wealth from the Americas, a wealth that stemmed from the commercial production of various tropical and subtropical commodities for sale in the Old World. In the short term, and with varying degrees of success, some English traders sought to feather their own nests by satisfying the labor needs of Spanish and Portuguese planters. A dual link began to form in the minds of the English, an association that was to exert a profound bearing on their designs for those islands in the eastern Caribbean that might be open to them to exploit. They realized first that commercial agriculture, the production of a range of highly prized staple crops, was one way of securing riches in this part of the New World and, second, that these riches were associated with the employment of a particular kind of workforce, enslaved West Africans. Not least because of its spatial proximity, the Iberian model, and particularly that of the Portuguese sugar producers of Brazil, was to exert an enormous influence on the English. Beginning in the mid-1620s the English used this model in their efforts to establish a foothold in the eastern Caribbean, not yet under Spanish or Portuguese domination. Initially, the English focused their attention on the Leeward and Windward Islands.

Those English people who, together with the Dutch and the French, made their way to the eastern Caribbean did not always behave in ways that conformed to Old World expectations of them. When it suited them to do so for pragmatic reasons, these different nationalities cooperated with one another in ways that were to have a direct bearing on the English decision, and ability, to employ enslaved African workers in their Caribbean possessions.

In 1624 a group of English settlers, mainly from East Anglia (a part of England that after 1630 would provide many of the New England colonists), landed on St. Christopher, or St. Kitts. The person who orchestrated this expedition, and who in 1626 was appointed by the Crown to be the Governor of the island, was Thomas Warner, a Puritan. During the 1630s and 1640s this Puritan connection would be of vital significance in the forging of trading links between New England and the English Caribbean. But that was for the future. In the short term Warner and his expedition were faced with three pressing problems: how to deal with the island's indigenous inhabitants, the Caribs; how to negotiate with the French, who were also interested in establishing a presence on St. Kitts; and how to make money.

Whatever Warner and his group may have hoped, the Caribs did not welcome them and their English civilization with open arms. Quite the contrary, in fact. In 1624 they tried, but failed, to throw these English newcomers off the island. The English were keenly aware of the threat posed by the Caribs and thus agreed to join forces with the French. A combined Anglo-French force defeated the Caribs, and in 1627 St. Kitts was formally, if somewhat uneasily, divided between the French and the English.

The settlers on St. Kitts assumed that the wealth they sought would come from commercial agriculture, and there was already an English model for them to emulate: Virginia. The future of Virginia was by no means assured at this early date, but, by the 1620s, money, a great deal of it, was being made from tobacco by those who were managing to hang on in the appalling epidemiological environment of the Tidewater Chesapeake. Tobacco prices were booming; the Old World seemed to be offering limitless markets for all the tobacco that the New World could supply. The English, and for that matter the French, settlers of St. Kitts had every reason to try to emulate Virginia and meet that demand.

During the 1630s the English tobacco producers of St. Kitts

and Virginia satisfied their labor requirements in exactly the same way: by the recruitment of indentured servants from the Old World. St. Kitts proved so attractive to this type of migrant that by 1635 there were already around 4,000 English people on the island. But herein lay the roots of a problem that would confront the English everywhere in the eastern Caribbean: the limited land resources of the Leeward and Windward Islands. Tobacco cultivation required land, lots of land, which the English managed to wrench from the indigenous population of St, Kitts. But, unlike the Chesapeake, St. Kitts did not have seemingly limitless tobacco lands. Indentured servants could not continue to be lured to St. Kitts by the promise of being able to secure land and freedom at the end of their term of service.

The initial success of St. Kitts, and the problems it posed, underpinned subsequent English expansion, and initially the expansion of tobacco, into the uninhabited islands of the Lesser Antilles. In 1628 the English began to settle on the island of Nevis. Roughly half of the first group of settlers came from England and Ireland, the other half came from St. Kitts. This pattern continued during the early 1630s, when the surplus population of St. Kitts helped to open up Montserrat and Antigua for the English. Later in the decade St. Kitts provided many of the early settlers of Tobago and St. Lucia.

Although the English tobacco producers of St. Kitts and these other islands continued to use indentured servants through the 1630s, they were also able to observe closehand an example of the use of enslaved African workers. Principally because of French policies regarding emigration, the French tobacco producers of St. Kitts were unable to secure the labor they needed from the Old World. The Dutch, who ran a slave trade from their island of St. Eustatius, were in a position to be able to offer them an alternative form of labor.

That the English too might be willing to use African workers was hinted at as early as 1626, when a merchant named Maurice Thompson landed sixty West Africans on St. Kitts. They were put to work alongside English indentured servants but not immediately decreed to be slaves. This state of affairs would change in a quite dramatic way during the 1640s and 1650s. This fundamental change, the transformation of the labor bases of the English Caribbean islands from the indentured servitude of Europeans to the involuntary servitude of West Africans, stemmed from the interaction of various economic, demographic, and ethnic factors that were operating both in the Caribbean and in the Old World. At the forefront of this transformation, but not the only island to experience it, was Barbados. By the 1660s the English had come to regard Barbados as being by far and away their most highly prized possession anywhere in the New World. The island's value to England, and the enormous wealth of a minority of its English inhabitants, hinged on the relationship that had been forged during the previous twenty years between sugar and slavery.

Barbados was claimed for the English in 1625 by Captain John Powell, who chanced upon it on his return to England from a trading expedition to Pernambuco, on the South American mainland. Once back in England, Powell soon persuaded Sir William Courteen, a wealthy merchant, to organize a joint stock company that would oversee the English settlement of Barbados. During the next few years there would be endless wrangles in England, which spilled over into Barbadian politics, about who actually owned the island. These acrimonious disputes did not seem to deter potential English migrants; by 1627 there were already around 1,200 of them in Barbados. Unlike their compatriots who made for St. Kitts, these migrants did not encounter an indigenous population. By the mid-1620s, for reasons that are not altogether clear, the native peoples who had once inhabited Barbados were extinct. Whatever plans the English forged for the island would not, and could not, be either threatened or furthered by an indigenous population. In fact, and not surprisingly so, English intentions for Barbados duplicated those that were being made simultaneously for St. Kitts.

Captain Powell, who from his trading ventures to the South American mainland had learned a good deal about the crops that could be grown in this part of the world, took with him to Barbados various plants and cuttings: Indian corn, yams, sweet potatoes, bananas, citrus fruits, cotton, indigo, and, something that would be of inestimable importance for the future, sugarcane. Not at all surprisingly in view of its success in Virginia, he also introduced tobacco. Anticipating the English lack of experience in producing these staple crops, Powell sought to draw on the expertise of the Arawak peoples of the South American mainland. He persuaded a group of them to accompany him to Barbados; within a decade of their arrival they would find themselves enslaved by the English settlers.

The first English settlers of Barbados were as fixated on tobacco as were their compatriots in the Tidewater Chesapeake. They had gone to Barbados in the expectation of making their fortunes and they had every intention of returning to England once those fortunes had been made. Even in 1630–31, when Barbados underwent its "starving time," the settlers who survived put all their efforts into tobacco cultivation, leaving the Arawaks to grow the basic foodstuffs they required. But there was one thing that stood between the settlers and the wealth they sought: land and labor they had, but the tobacco they grew was of such poor quality that it often rotted before reaching European markets. By the early 1630s it was already apparent that the route to wealth lay not in tobacco but in the production of an alternative staple crop.

Sugarcane was not immediately seized upon by the settlers as the answer. First they experimented with cotton, and by 1640 that commodity was equal in value to tobacco as an export crop. By the late 1630s, however, thanks mainly to the experiments conducted by two planters, James Holip and James Drax, sugar was being grown on a commercial scale in Barbados. As one commentator reported in 1643, "Barbados is grown the most flourishing island in all these American parts, and I verily believe in all the world, for the production of sugar." During the next twenty years the production of sugar became truly phenomenal. In a single year, between August 1664 and August 1665, Barbados exported twenty-eight million pounds of sugar. By this time almost 90 percent of the island's exports consisted of raw sugar or such sugar products as rum and molasses. Barbados could indeed stake a claim to being the "Jewel in the Crown" of the English empire in the New World. But the "Sugar Revolution" that occurred during the 1640s and 1650s (a heightened English demand for sugar and the ability of Barbados to satisfy that demand) created a need for labor on a scale, and of a type, that the Old World was both unable and increasingly unwilling to supply.

As with tobacco and cotton, it took the English some time to learn how to cultivate and process sugarcane, and they obtained much of the knowledge they sought from the well-established Brazilian sugar industry. They also learned about the dependence of that industry upon enslaved West African workers. From the beginning Captain Powell had thought in terms of employing West Africans in Barbados, and it was thanks to him that by 1627 around fifty of them had been brought to the island. But through the 1630s and into the 1640s the labor needs of planters continued to be satisfied by English indentured servants. They were attracted to Barbados for precisely the same reasons that continued to attract other migrants to St. Kitts and the Tidewater Chesapeake.

By 1638, on the eve of the Sugar Revolution, the population of Barbados numbered about 6,000. Approximately one-third of them were servants, only about 200 of them of African descent. This situation would change beyond recognition during the course of the next twenty years. By 1660 there were 26,200 Europeans and 27,100 West Africans in Barbados. A similar transformation was evident in the other English islands, as they too came to place an ever-increasing reliance on sugar production. By 1660 Nevis had a slight West African majority; West Africans accounted for fractionally under half of the Antiguan population and for almost 44 percent of that of St. Kitts.

Given what they had learned about the status and treatment of West Africans in Brazil; their pressing labor requirements; a Dutch willingness to satisfy those requirements; and their unslaked thirst for wealth, it is not particularly surprising that the sugar planters of the English Caribbean acted in the way they did. If nothing else, economic rationality dictated that West Africans were the most profitable form of labor currently available. Indeed, it would have been more surprising had English sugar planters not looked to West Africa for the large, fixed workforces they considered necessary for the efficient and profitable operation of their plantations. If they felt they needed any other justifications for their actions, and there is no suggestion that they did, they could find it in the negative images of Africans that had become so firmly entrenched in the English consciousness during the course of the previous century.

The disruptions wrought by the English Civil War, and the upturn in English wage levels during the early 1640s, served to diminish the flow and increase the cost of indentured servants from England. There was another source of European labor available, however: the Irish. Through the 1640s and early 1650s, poor crops and high rates of unemployment, conditions that were not helped by the long-standing English attempt to civilize Ireland, forced many Irish into indentured servitude in Barbados.

These Roman Catholic newcomers, culturally scorned and despised by the English, were put to backbreaking labor in the cane fields. They were worked so long and hard that the English sometimes referred to them as "white slaves." But despite their appalling treatment, and possibly because of the ultimate protection afforded them by their Christianity and their white skin, the Irish in Barbados were never legally enslaved by the English.

The Brazilian sugar industry provided the English in Barbados with a model of how they might resolve their pressing labor problems; the Dutch provided them with the means of doing so. It was in this context that the location of Barbados came into play. By the 1640s and 1650s the Dutch had long been established in the transatlantic slave trade, and, if there seemed to be a marketing opportunity, their routes from West Africa to the New World could very easily take them via Barbados. Barbados was a much shorter distance from the slaving ports of West Africa than were the islands of the Western Caribbean, or even the Leeward and Windward Islands. The Dutch had every reason to offer their services to the labor-hungry sugar planters of Barbados, and the latter to accept them. The Dutch offered apparently limitless supplies of workers; they provided generous credit arrangements; and they could also transport Barbadian sugar to Old World markets.

There is no suggestion that Barbadian sugar planters thought twice, or even thought much at all, before turning to the Dutch to satisfy their labor requirements. Neither is there any suggestion that they wrestled for very long with the problem of devising a suitable economic and legal status for the African workers supplied to them by the Dutch. These were essentially profit-motivated, pragmatic men who, even if they were aware of them, were disinclined to spend their time debating abstract English concepts of enslavement. They were in desperate need of workers; those being offered to them were cheaper than indentured European servants and had long been enslaved in the New World's other sugar economies. There seemed no good reason, economic or otherwise, for Barbadian planters to turn their backs on the workforce that they were being offered by the Dutch. Moreover, there also seemed to be no compelling reason why this workforce should not be an enslaved workforce.

It was certainly the case that through the middle years of the seventeenth century, during the Sugar Revolution, the cost of acquiring an African worker for life was greater than that of securing the services of an indentured European servant for a limited term. However, that differential shrank dramatically as the flow of indentured European servants to Barbados dwindled during the 1640s. Barbadian sugar planters were also beginning to identify other financial advantages that might be reaped from the use of enslaved Africans. The maintenance costs associated with slave labor would be somewhat lower than those associated with indentured servants. West Africans, planters came to believe, could be fed and clothed far more cheaply than could indentured Europeans, who retained some degree of bargaining power. Moreover, planters were under no real constraints when it came to the physical coercion of their West African workers. Far more work could be extracted from West

Africans on an hourly, daily, weekly, and yearly basis than it ever could be from Europeans. Indeed, the prices that planters were receiving for their sugar were such that, if they so chose, they could afford to work Africans to death and replenish them as and when the need to do so arose. So the high mortality rates of newly arrived West Africans—as many as one in three were likely to die within three years of reaching Barbados— did not deter English sugar planters. West Africans offered them something that Europeans, including the Irish whom they so despised, did not: the prospect of an assured, perpetual, and productive workforce. This much at least was clear to them from their knowledge of Brazil's slave system.

Barbadian planters were thoroughly familiar with the Brazilian model of enslavement and, even before the Sugar Revolution, some thought it might be applicable to Barbados. In 1636 Governor Henry Hawley and his Council deliberated the precise legal status of the Arawaks and the small number of West Africans on the island. They declared quite categorically that unless a prior contract of employment had been drawn up, all "Negroes and Indians that came here to be sold [would] serve for life." This was the earliest pronouncement anywhere in English America that both West Africans and native Americans might be legitimately enslaved. The economic practice of the 1640s and 1650s, which became enshrined in law during the early 1660s, ensured that a lifelong and heritable servitude would be the lot of those West Africans who were being brought in ever-increasing numbers to Barbados.

That this was so reflected the pragmatic needs of the planters who orchestrated the Sugar Revolution. These were men who had previously tried their hand as tobacco and cotton producers; men who, with the profits they had made from these crops, together perhaps with some credit from the Dutch, could afford to make the heavy capital investment in the equipment needed to process sugar for the market, as well as to acquire the land and labor they needed to expand their operations. Richard Ligon, who visited Barbados during the height of the Sugar Revolution, estimated that it cost about £14,000 to get a sugar plantation up and running. Only already established planters had access to this kind of capital.

One problem that the elite planter-politicans could not re-solve was that land was in comparatively short supply. Barbados measured only fourteen by twenty-one miles. There were clearly defined limits on the expansion of sugar cultivation, even by those who could afford it, and there was not enough land to hold out as a continuing lure to prospective migrants from the Old World.

The English Civil War interrupted the flow of indentured servants to Barbados, a flow that was never to be fully resumed in the postwar years. The fact that by 1650 Barbadian planters were already turning to West Africans to resolve their labor problems did not help matters. Barbados had come to enjoy a glowing reputation in the eyes of those English interests who derived a financial benefit from it: from the taxes that, to the increasing disquiet and disgust of Barbadian planters, could be heaped on sugar to the money made by those who shipped that commodity to England and who, in return, supplied the con-sumer goods considered necessary by eminent planters to es-tablish the material culture of their "Little England" in the Caribbean. As Henry Whistler, an Englishman who visited the island in the mid-1650s, commented, Barbados "is one of the richest spots of ground in the world." Another European visitor to the Barbados of the 1650s, Father Antoine Biet, con-firmed that "extravagance is very great among these parts." En-glish planters, Biet asserted, had one motive only for being in

Barbados: "They come here in order to be wealthy." But by no means all those who made for the island achieved that goal.

As the census taken in 1680 so clearly demonstrates, wealth had become concentrated in the hands of a small minority of planters. About 175 planters, or roughly 7 percent of the property owners listed in the census, virtually monopolized the island's wealth. These men, most of whom were descendants of those who had settled in Barbados during the 1630s, exercised an iron grip on every aspect of life and would stop at nothing to maintain their hegemony. They were in close proximity to, and felt themselves to be under continuous threat from, an enslaved population that heavily outnumbered them. They sought to secure their physical safety, and their continuing wealth from sugar production, by resorting to the most barbaric treatment of their African workforces.

Sugar planters took several steps to prevent organized resistance. They deliberately separated newly imported Africans from others from the same regions and, in the process, disrupted family and kinship networks that could have formed the building blocks of widespread rebellion. They ruthlessly suppressed the traditional religious beliefs and practices of West Africans, not with a view to replacing them with Christianity but because they represented alternative value systems that might act as a unifying force within the slave quarters. But Christianity would be assigned a significant role by planters in their attempt to secure docile, submissive workforces.

The planter class was constantly reassured by the local Anglican clergy, as well as by the Anglican hierarchy in London, that there was no inconsistency whatsoever between Christianity and bondage, that slaveholding was perfectly legitimate. However, there were those among the clergy, most famously Morgan Godwyn, who sought to remind them of their obligations as Christian masters and mistresses and suggested that it would be very much to their secular advantage if they proselytized their bondpeople. Christian slaves, argued Godwyn, would be infused with the values of the ideal Christian servant: loyalty, obedience, and diligence. The Anglican planters of Barbados rejected this argument out of hand. They knew full well that the maintenance of their regime depended not upon constructing a common, shared religious ideology with their slaves, which at the very least would acknowledge the humanity of West Africans, but upon maintaining difference. In fact, the slaves did not particularly care to subscribe to the religious belief system of those who had enslaved them, but sugar planters were determined to prevent their being offered that opportunity. As a potentially unifying ideology, Christianity in the slave quarters was considered by planters to be just as dangerous as traditional West African belief systems. Moreover, Christianity raised another dangerous possibility: the forging of links between nonelite whites and enslaved people who subscribed to a common religion.

The planter elite of Barbados sought in other ways to distance itself from what it depicted as the totally uncivilized, irredeemable culture of West Africans. Planters employed a language and behavior deliberately designed to debase their enslaved workers and to deny their humanity. But the cultural superiority that the planter class was so very desperate to establish was also expressed quite explicitly in another way, in their material culture. Eminent planters sought reassurance, protection even, in English cultural models, and they were making enough money from sugar to be able to import that culture wholesale. With much of the food they ate and many of the clothes they wore, most imported from England, and with the houses they lived in, sugar planters aped elite English

culture in a manner that was entirely inappropriate to the physical environment in which they lived. But planters considered
this ostentatious display of wealth, which sometimes shocked
European visitors to Barbados, essential to their cultural domination. English civilization was defined for them largely in material terms, and it was a civilization that they intended would
remain forever inaccessible to people of West African descent.
But by the 1670s and 1680s it was also a civilization that was
inaccessible to the vast majority of Europeans who lived in
Barbados, as well as to those who contemplated emigrating
there from the Old World.

There were several reasons why the English people who in
earlier years might have contemplated embarking for Barbados
as indentured servants stayed away after 1650. The reputation
that the island had secured for itself as it underwent its Sugar
Revolution was anything but glowing. Reports reached England
of the arduous and often dangerous work involved in sugar
production, of the amounts of labor insisted upon by sugar
planters, and of the physical coercion they were willing to resort to in order to secure that labor. Moreover, because land
was so scarce and consequently so expensive to acquire, Barbados seemed to offer few postindenture opportunities. A vi-
cious circle was effected. Shortages of indentured European
servants encouraged sugar planters to turn to enslaved African
workers who were coerced in ways that prospective European
servants found demeaning and unacceptable when applied to
themselves. Those who had a choice of New World destinations
deliberately avoided Barbados, thereby persuading planters to
purchase yet more West Africans.

The second half of the seventeenth century witnessed a dramatic increase in the size of Barbados's enslaved population
and an equally dramatic decline in the number of people of

European ancestry on the island. Between 1660 and 1710 that number halved from 26,000 to around 13,000. This steep drop was indicative not of a demographic calamity but of migration from Barbados. Those who could afford to do so often retired to England. Those for whom this was not an option, and for whom Barbados seemed to hold fewer and fewer opportunities, left the island. That they wished, or felt themselves forced, to do so was a direct result of the overpopulation of Barbados. That so many people were able to leave the island in the expectation of bettering themselves elsewhere in the New World was made possible by the English conquest of Jamaica in 1655 and, a decade later, by the founding of a new English colony on the North American mainland.

By no means all those in the lower reaches of Barbadian society chose, or were able, to leave the island. Some who remained were drawn into the island's slave system as overseers and managers. Others, many others, were left to eke out a precarious existence at the very margins of white society. By the 1660s, though, in a manner reminiscent of St. Kitts thirty years earlier, an overpopulated Barbados stood poised to provide a pool of settlers for England's two new colonies of Jamaica and Carolina.

For a combination of commercial and military reasons England had long hoped to secure a permanent presence in the western Caribbean. Those hopes began to be realized during the 1640s when, against the backdrop of heightened Anglo-Spanish tensions in the Old World, an English expeditionary force of 1,000 men, under the command of a Captain Jackson, attempted to invade Jamaica. Although this Spanish-held island was not very heavily fortified, Jackson's force was repelled. Despite this setback the English did not give up on their aim of establishing themselves in this part of the Americas.

In 1655 the English organized another expeditionary force, this time 2,500 men under the joint command of Admiral William Penn and Richard Venables, which was designed to seize control of all the Spanish possessions in the western Caribbean. From the English standpoint it did not particularly matter which of the Spanish islands was taken first: Cuba, Hispaniola, and Jamaica would each have provided a base from which to launch further assaults on the Spanish empire. Principally because of its well-established sugar economy, and thereby the instant wealth as well as the strategic possibilities it was thought to offer, Hispaniola was Venables and Penn's prime target. They were to encounter rather more than they had bargained for. Hispaniola was very well defended, and the English failed to take it. Convinced that further assaults on the island would be futile, the English turned their attention to Jamaica. Jamaica was less well fortified than Hispaniola, and the island was captured by the English with comparative ease. Penn and Venables had managed to secure for England an immensely valuable base in the western Caribbean, but not an island whose economy was flourishing.

While Jamaica was under Spanish rule, its main economic importance had lain not in the cultivation of lucrative staple crops but in its livestock industry. There was no instant wealth to be seized by the English invaders, and such was their frustration that they behaved in a manner that only compounded their problems. Ordinary English soldiers, who were described by one contemporary as being "common cheats, thieves, cutpurses, and such like lewd persons," laid waste to the land. They were hardly adequate founders of the permanent settlement the English knew would be necessary to retain Jamaica. Indeed, the soldiers were such reluctant farmers that they even refused to grow enough to feed themselves and had to be provisioned from England. One of the few, but highly significant, points in their favor was that in 1656 they helped to foil a Spanish attempt to reconquer Jamaica.

Oliver Cromwell appreciated that if Jamaica was going to be successfully defended against subsequent Spanish attacks, and become of any economic worth to England, then large numbers of English people had to be encouraged to migrate there. This encouragement came in the shape of land grants, exemptions from customs duties, and the promise that the children born to English parents in Jamaica would enjoy all the rights and liberties of freeborn English people. These promises, and particularly perhaps the offer of land on generous terms, proved highly successful in attracting migrants to Jamaica, not only from England but also from other parts of English America.

From the Barbadian perspective the English seizure of Jamaica was a godsend. To those in the lower reaches of that island's white society Jamaica offered the prospect of land ownership, of freedom, of economic advancement. Established planters who wished to expand their operations, or to set up their younger sons as sugar producers, believed that they would be able to do so in Jamaica. During the last three decades of the seventeenth century Barbados would provide a steady stream of settlers for Jamaica, settlers who took to that island their knowledge of sugar and slavery. The coastal regions of Jamaica offered the prospect of potentially rich sugar lands, but initially it would be to the sea rather than to the land that the first settlers would look for the wealth they sought in the western Caribbean.

Assuming always that they could retain it, the English considered Jamaica an ideal base from which they could launch privateering raids against the Spanish. Privateering entailed some capital investment and some degree of risk, but it held out the prospect of fabulous wealth, a wealth that it might take years to accumulate from any form of commercial agriculture, including sugar production. It was only during the 1670s, when England and Spain were trying to repair their relationship, that attempts were made to outlaw an activity that was becoming increasingly embarrassing to the English government.

Privateering delayed Jamaica's Sugar Revolution by some years, but it also provided a vitally important source of the capital needed to effect that revolution. During the 1670s and 1680s some attempts were made to develop Jamaica's agricultural potential. Planters began the production of what are sometimes referred to as the "minor" staple crops—ginger, cotton, and coffee—and these commodities continued to feature in the Jamaican economy. But drawing heavily upon Barbadian expertise, they also began to grow sugarcane, and by the turn of the seventeenth century sugar was well on the way toward becoming Jamaica's most highly prized export. Unlike Barbados, however, Jamaican agriculture never became a monoculture, with all the financial risks that this could entail.

Given the Barbadian connection, it was entirely predictable that Jamaica's sugar planters would turn to enslaved Africans to provide the workforces they required. And turn they did. In 1660 the island's population of around 3,000 included approximately 500 people of African descent. Just thirteen years later that number had grown to 9,500. Thereafter the size of Jamaica's enslaved population would increase in direct proportion to the intensity of the island's Sugar Revolution. By 1710 there were 58,000 Africans in Jamaica, accounting for almost 90 percent of the island's population. By the early eighteenth century Jamaica was poised to emulate the reputation of Barbados as England's most valuable American possession.

By the 1660s and 1670s Jamaica was providing an obvious,

if somewhat geographically distant, solution to the difficulties being experienced by Barbados. But during these same decades another, equally distant solution to these difficulties would be presented on the North American mainland. These years saw the founding of a new colony, Carolina, that would be as much a Barbadian as it was an English creation. During the latter part of the seventeenth century all the imperatives that informed the already deeply entrenched slave society of Barbados would be transported wholesale, and uncritically, to the Carolina Lowcountry.

The entire region that lay between Virginia in the north and Spanish Florida in the south had long been of interest to the English. Some saw there the prospect of developing a fur trade comparable with that of the northern frontier; others were tempted by what seemed to be an ideal physical environment in which to cultivate highly prized staple crops; and, of course, there was the continuing interest in establishing bases from which to launch attacks on Spanish America. By the end of the 1640s, a sign perhaps of diminishing postindenture opportunities in the Tidewater Chesapeake, some English settlers had already migrated to the areas around Albemarle Sound, to the region that subsequently became part of North Carolina. Albemarle Sound, however, flattered to deceive. Unlike Chesapeake Bay, it did not provide easy access for the planters who established themselves close to its shores. They had little alternative but to ship their tobacco via the Chesapeake. This part of Carolina would prove far less alluring to potential migrants, especially from Barbados, than the area farther south, the area that the English came to refer to as the Lowcountry.

Sir Peter Colleton was probably the first person to appreciate that the Lowcountry would form an invaluable commercial and military addition to England's American possessions at the same time as it could help to resolve the Barbadian problem of European overpopulation. Colleton, a Royalist during the English Civil War, had spent some time exiled in Barbados. Someone else who appreciated the potential value of the Low-country, and who was a friend of Colleton's, was Governor William Berkeley of Virginia. Berkeley and Colleton needed the sanction and support of England for their proposed new colony, and, with the Restoration of King Charles II in 1660, they found the backing they sought in abundant supply in London.

The King was attracted to Colleton and Berkeley's proposal by the additional customs revenues that were likely to accrue from the creation of a new American colony. He was also keen to find a way of rewarding those in his circle who had supported him during the years of Civil War and his long exile from England. This could be done, he came to believe, at no cost to himself by offering them vast acreages of land in the colony being proposed by Colleton and Berkeley. With the support of the King safely secured, Colleton and Berkeley had little difficulty in enlisting the enthusiastic backing of some of the most influential men in England for their scheme. In 1663 a group that included the Earls of Clarendon and Craven, Lord Ashley, Sir George Carteret and the Duke of Albemarle, as well as Colleton and Berkeley, successfully petitioned the Crown for a charter that would authorize them to colonize the entire region to the south of Virginia. It was to be the southern portion of this enormous land grant that would be of most interest to prospective migrants from Barbados.

Following an abortive attempt in 1665 to establish a settlement in the vicinity of Port Royal, the English colonization of the Carolina Lowcountry finally got under way four years later. From the outset the Barbadian connection would be of paramount importance. The fleet set sail from England in 1669 and called in at Barbados to collect men, supplies, and—highly reminiscent of Captain Powell almost fifty years earlier—seeds and plants to try out in the Carolina environment. Meanwhile, back in London, the Carolina Proprietors were devising a scheme for the settlement and government of their colony. The blueprint drafted in 1669 by the Earl of Shaftesbury and his secretary, the political theorist John Locke—the "Fundamental Constitutions" for Carolina—was idealistic and anachronistic in the extreme. It was one of the most utopian schemes ever designed by Englishmen for the New World, but, at the same time, it could not help reflecting the pragmatic interests of the Carolina Proprietors.

The Carolina Proprietors realized that if they were to make money from their lands in the New World then they must find ways of attracting settlers to their colony. This they believed they could do by offering prospective migrants land grants on generous terms, freedom of religious worship, and English rights and liberties. But, and clearly with an eye on Barbados, they also thought it both appropriate and necessary to offer the settlers of Carolina something else: security of their property rights. Barbadian planters who contemplated moving to the Lowcountry were being guaranteed the continuance of the right they were already claiming for themselves to hold a particular form of property: enslaved West Africans.

This section of the Fundamental Constitutions, which owed much to Locke, demonstrated quite clearly the importance that the English attached to their plantation colonies. But it also demonstrated something else: the ways in which late-seventeenth-century English thinkers were legitimating the institution of slavery. Whatever else it may have entailed, the English Civil War, its origins and its immediate aftermath, involved a fierce debate in England about the rights and liberties of Englishmen. Indeed, much of the political discourse of mid- and late-seventeenth-century England focused on questions of rights, freedoms, and obligations. These were the not always theoretical political issues that divided English people of the period. But it was out of, and in the context of, these discourses that thinkers such as Locke felt obliged to consider the antithesis of English freedom and liberty: enslavement. How might slavery be legitimated?

For Locke the answer to this question lay in his understanding of the social contract that underpinned political society. Despite his ideas about inalienable personal rights, which significantly included the right to property, Locke was able to justify the institution of slavery by arguing that it lay outside the realm of the social contract. Slavery, he argued, resembled warfare in that it involved the opposing forces of slave and master. In this respect slavery was no different from any other war: it entailed the suspension of all normal social relationships. Moreover, there were those who, because of their lack of virtue or because they lacked a propertied interest, could never qualify for participation in political society. Such an argument did not necessarily single out West Africans or, for that matter, native Americans as the only groups eligible for enslavement, but it was one that could be employed to legitimate their bondage. Indeed, together with the religious dimensions of the abstract English concept of slavery, it was an argument that, over the years, would come to find great favor among the slaveholders of English America.

In the short term, however, the Carolina settlers, and particularly those from Barbados, were far more swayed by the property rights they were being assured of than they were any theoretical justification of those rights. Above all else, the early

settlers of Carolina, especially those from Barbados, were prag-
matists. They regarded slaveholding as being both a necessary
and a desirable prerequisite for the successful exploitation of
the Lowcountry and its resources.

From the beginning the Carolina Lowcountry represented
an extension of Barbados to the North American mainland. For
many years the economic life of the Lowcountry would be ori-
ented toward Barbados rather than toward either England or
the other mainland colonies. Commercial agriculture featured
prominently in the plans of the English and Barbadian founders
of Carolina, and as early as the 1660s rice had been mentioned
as a possible export crop. It was only around the turn of the
seventeenth century, however, and not least because of the
prior experience of rice cultivation brought there by enslaved
West Africans, that rice began to figure prominently in the
Lowcountry economy. It would be another twenty or thirty
years before rice began to provide Carolina planters with a
wealth virtually unknown elsewhere in the North American
mainland, a wealth that bore some comparison with the vast
incomes of West Indian sugar planters.

During the last three decades of the seventeenth century the
Carolina settlers secured far more modest incomes from various other economic activities that provided employment for the
enslaved people they had brought with them from Barbados,
economic activities that generated a steady demand for more
slaves. Reflective of the Barbadian link, many of these activities
were geared to supplying the needs of the English sugar colonies. Timber was required, especially in Barbados (which had
been virtually deforested in the quest for sugar lands), for fuel,
building, and making the casks and barrels in which sugar and
sugar products were shipped to market. Because of the pre-
mium that attached to sugar cultivation, the islands needed

grains and meats and other basic foodstuffs. Very quickly a thriving trade developed between Charleston and the English West Indies. In return for their timber and foodstuffs, Carolina merchants received sugar and sugar products. These items, together with the pelts and furs that also formed a highly important sector of the early Carolina economy, were traded for English manufactured goods.

The Caribbean connection was vitally important to the Lowcountry for another reason: it supplied much of the enslaved labor that the Carolina settlers had always deemed essential for their economic operations in this corner of the New World. From the beginning enslaved West Africans were employed in all sectors of the Carolina economy, and well before rice became entrenched as the Lowcountry's major staple crop in the 1720s and 1730s, slaves were being brought there in ever-increasing numbers. By 1708, for example, Carolina's population of 8,000 already included 4,000 people of African descent. By 1720 this proportion had increased to almost 60 percent; by the 1730s, when rice cultivation soared in importance, it had reached around 66 percent. Of all the colonies planted by the English in mainland North America, only one, Carolina, would have a black majority.

The work routines in the Carolina Lowcountry, both before and after rice rose to prominence, were somewhat different from those involved in sugar production. But in no small part because of the Caribbean connection, the exploitation of the enslaved workforces of the Lowcountry was just as ruthless as it was in the English sugar islands. Neither was it any coincidence, nor particularly surprising, that when the Barbadian émigrés who rose quickly to political prominence in Carolina determined that the time had come to enact a comprehensive slave code, they should have looked to Barbados for their model. In its form, content, and intentions, in some of the language it employed, the code that they devised in 1696 was strikingly similar to that drawn up by the planter-politicians of Barbados in the early 1660s.

The enslavement of West Africans in Barbados could not have been predicted with absolute certainty when Captain Powell first set foot on the island. However, given the circumstances of the 1640s and 1650s, it would have been highly surprising had the English settlers of Barbados, these pragmatic, profit-driven people, not turned to enslaved West African workers during these years. Something else that could have been predicted with equal certainty by 1660 was that those who left Barbados to seek their fortunes in Jamaica and Carolina would take with them their firm commitment to the institution of slavery.

The first English settlers of St. Kitts and Barbados had not left the Old World with the explicit intention of securing their freedom, their advancement, by enslaving others. Within a decade or so of their arrival in the Caribbean, however, they were already associating their material betterment with the employment of enslaved West Africans. Their awareness of the Spanish and Portuguese models of slavery, the difficulties they encountered in securing a sufficient number of European workers to man their plantations, and the ready availability of a constant supply of West Africans courtesy of Dutch slave traders were all instrumental in effecting such a rapid transformation of the labor base of England's Caribbean possessions. That transformation, in its turn, would have both practical and ideological consequences for the Chesapeake colonies. It would provide them not only with additional models of slave systems but also, and significantly, with models that had been devised not by the Spanish or by the Portuguese but by their fellow countrymen. Moreover, these same slave systems would play a crucial part in determining the exact timing of the transformation of their own labor bases from a dependence upon indentured European to involuntary West African servitude.

4

Tobacco Slaves: The Chesapeake Colonies

The social and economic blueprint devised by the Virginia Company for its proposed colony in the Chesapeake in many ways continued the assumptions and imperatives that had informed the settlement at Roanoke. The company's intention was to forge lucrative trading links with the indigenous peoples of the region who, in their turn, would derive many cultural and material benefits from their association with the English. If a water route could be found to the Orient, then so much the better.

Initially neither the Virginia Company nor those who settled at Jamestown envisaged that agriculture would contribute much to the wealth they expected to extract from the Chesapeake. But, regardless of their Old World status and occupational experience, the settlers would be required to perform some agricultural labor. To begin with they would be provisioned by the company, but they were expected to support themselves within a matter of a few months. The settlers would have to do enough agricultural labor to feed themselves but, it was assumed both in London and in Jamestown, most of their time and energies would be devoted to other profit-making activities. Commercial agriculture, with all that it entailed in terms of land and labor requirements, did not feature in the original English design for Virginia.

From the beginning, servitude was an integral aspect of the English design for Virginia. In keeping with traditional English practice, the Virginia Company devised a scheme that promised them close control over anticipated profits. The early settlers were contracted to work for the company for a seven-year term, at the end of which they would be eligible for a share of the company's profits. Initially the company did not envisage private economic enterprise or offer the prospect of freedom in the shape of land ownership.

The high hopes of the company and the settlers were quickly dashed by the reality of the Chesapeake environment. The instant wealth that had been hoped for simply did not materialize; the first settlers died like flies from the unfamiliar diseases of the Jamestown area; those who remained alive were often too debilitated or, because of the comparatively high social status they had enjoyed in the Old World, too proud to work, even to feed themselves. That the settlement established at Jamestown actually survived at all owed much to the material assistance provided by Powhatan and his people, to the strict discipline imposed on the surviving settlers by Captain John Smith, and, in London, to the determination of the Virginia Company to persist in its quest for profits.

In its early days the Virginia Company proved remarkably successful in attracting settlers and investment capital. This success owed something to the company's glowing promotional literature, but it also reflected the willingness of the company to make fundamental alterations to its original design. In the 1610s, the company introduced a package of reforms that exerted a profound, and persistent, influence on every aspect of life in Virginia.

Two of these reforms had to do with land, and, given traditional English concepts of freedom, they were to have a crucial political, as well as a purely economic, bearing on the subsequent course of Virginia's history. First, potential English investors who had no intention of crossing the Atlantic were offered enormous land grants in exchange for their financial capital. It was left entirely to them when those grants would be settled and who would settle them. Second, and of immediate relevance to those already in Virginia, land was privatized. Previously the settlers had been required to work on lands owned by the Virginia Company; now they would be permitted to work on lands of their own. In the English understanding of the term, they were being granted their freedom. The translation of this freedom into political reality was effected by another monumental reform introduced by the Virginia Company: the ending of autocratic rule in Virginia and the inauguration of representative government. As in England, participation in that government, the right to vote and to hold office, would be firmly rooted in the ownership of land. Virginia's new elective assembly, the House of Burgesses, convened for the first time in the summer of 1619.

It was by chance rather than by design that these reforms coincided with, and facilitated, a fundamental change in economic direction. When allied with the reforms introduced by the Virginia Company, this change of economic direction was to radically reshape the relationship between the English colonists and the indigenous population of the Chesapeake. It would also provide the context, the framework, within which the enslavement of West Africans would proceed during the remainder of the seventeenth century.

By the early 1610s it was as clear to the settlers who were persisting at Jamestown as it was to the Virginia Company in London that if profits were to be made in the Chesapeake they were not likely to come from precious metals. John Smith's exploration of the Chesapeake's waterways offered little hope of a passage to the Orient, at least not in the foreseeable future. Some money was to be made from trading with local native Americans but nowhere near the profits that the settlers had imagined would enable them to return to England, there to live a life of affluence. It became increasingly apparent to the colonists at Jamestown that the wealth they sought would have to come from other sources, from the exploitation of a natural resource or the production of a commodity that they could market in the Old World. By the mid-1610s, after some experimentation with what to them was an unfamiliar crop, the settlers had discovered the commodity they sought, a commodity that was greatly in demand in Europe: tobacco. From this point onward commercial agriculture would form the basis of the prosperity that the Virginia Company and the settlers had always sought in the Chesapeake.

By 1617 Jamestown was caught up in a tobacco-producing frenzy. Governor Samuel Argall, who arrived in Jamestown that year, was surprised and appalled by what he found there. Far from being an ordered and orderly settlement of "civilized" English people, Jamestown consisted of "but five or six houses, the church down, the palizados broken, the bridge in pieces, the well of fresh water spoiled, the store-house they used for the church, the market-place, and streets, and all other spare places planted with tobacco—the colony dispersed, all about planting tobacco." Nothing could dissuade the settlers from putting all their energies into tobacco production: not Argall's displeasure, not King James's opposition to the smoking of tobacco on moral grounds, and not the dire warnings from some in the Virginia Company of the potential dangers implicit in monoculture.

By 1620, two things stood between the Virginia settlers and the profits they sought from tobacco: land and the labor to work that land. As far as land was concerned, the problem was not, as it would be for the English in the Caribbean, a finite amount of that commodity. If nothing else, John Smith's explorations had suggested to the settlers that the land they needed for tobacco production was abundantly available. The problem was that the land they sought was already occupied. Moreover, continuous tobacco cultivation rapidly depleted the soil. From the colonists' perspective, even had their skills in animal husbandry permitted it, and had they been prepared to engage in crop rotation, there was no financial incentive whatsoever to try to improve their exhausted tobacco fields. The land they needed to start tobacco production anew was all around them; that land was in possession of native Americans.

By 1620 the colonists were simply taking the acres they required for their expanding tobacco economy without even the pretense of negotiation or payment. Increasing encroachments on native American lands, and especially onto their hunting grounds, largely accounted for the deterioration of relations between the English and the indigenous populations of the Tidewater Chesapeake that finally exploded in 1622. What is usually referred to as the "Massacre of 1622," the native American attack that resulted in the death of 347 English settlers and almost wiped out Jamestown, gave the colonists the excuse they needed to take even more of what they wanted from the indigenous population of the Chesapeake.

As far as the survivors of the Massacre of 1622 were concerned, by virtue of launching this unprovoked assault native Americans had forfeited any legal and moral rights they might previously have claimed to the ownership of the lands they occupied. As one contemporary settler explained, in words that

echoed the comments of late-sixteenth-century English propagandists, "we, who hitherto have had possession of no more
ground than their waste and our purchase at a valuable consideration to their own contentment . . . may now by right of war,
and law of nations, invade the country, and those who sought
to destroy us: whereby we shall enjoy their cultivated places."
The English no longer felt themselves under any obligation to
negotiate for, let alone to pay for, the tobacco lands they
sought; they claimed every justification for taking those lands
by force, for dispossessing and, if necessary, for exterminating
the native Americans who occupied those lands. During the
remainder of the seventeenth century the twin processes of
dispossession and extermination were to be hastened in a way
that the English had neither anticipated nor intended. They
had succumbed in the hundreds in what for them was the
disease-ridden environment of the Tidewater Chesapeake. In
their turn, native Americans had no natural immunity to the
diseases that crossed the Atlantic with the English and other
Europeans. What to the inhabitants of the Old World were
such innocuous ailments as measles and mumps devastated the
indigenous populations of the New World.

The land for tobacco cultivation, then, was there if the English had the military means to take it, and, over the course of
the seventeenth century, take it they did. But as of the late
1610s and 1620s the aspiring tobacco producers of the Tidewater Chesapeake were confronted by a second problem that
was acting as a brake on their profits. That problem had to do
with their labor requirements, with the large workforces they
reckoned necessary for successful tobacco cultivation. There
was no way in which those labor requirements could be satisfied by Virginia's existing English population, a population that
had almost been wiped out in 1622; a population that, despite

the importing of women to Virginia as wives for the settlers, showed no sign of growing by natural increase; and a population that continued to be devastated by diseases to which as yet the settlers had no immunity. The Massacre of 1622 was followed in 1623 by what those who survived it described as the "Great Mortality." So many settlers died from ailments of one sort or another, and so many others were debilitated by them, that, according to one contemporary, the living were hardly able to bury the dead. Probably between 500 and 600 colonists fell victim to the Great Mortality. Between 1607 and 1624 about 7,600 people had emigrated from England to Virginia. By 1624, after almost twenty years of settlement, Virginia's English population totaled approximately 1,200.

Neither the Massacre of 1622 nor the Great Mortality of the following year quenched the colonists' enthusiasm for tobacco production. But both episodes further complicated the labor problem. As one settler, John Pory, pointed out, "Our principall wealth consisteth in our servants." By 1620 or thereabouts, three sources of labor were available for consideration by Virginia's tobacco producers: native Americans, indentured servants from the Old World, and West Africans.

On the face of it, if only because they were there on the spot, native Americans would seem to have been a logical choice of workforce for Virginia's burgeoning tobacco economy. A few voices were raised in the aftermath of the Massacre of 1622 suggesting the advantages of coercing the native Americans into working the tobacco fields rather than exterminating them. Such a line of argument never attracted widespread support in Virginia, and the question is, why not?

Certain elements of the negative stereotyping of native Americans by sixteenth-century English commentators raised the theoretical possibility of their enslavement; more flattering images, combined with the pragmatic roles that English writers devised for them, militated against such an eventuality. After the Massacre of 1622, however, these flattering images had little influence. We must therefore look to pragmatic rather than ideological reasons for the colonists' choosing to exterminate, not enslave, native Americans.

The indigenous populations of the Chesapeake were not densely settled and could not be easily subjugated by the English, given the manpower at their disposal. The English might enjoy a superiority of weaponry, but through the middle years of the seventeenth century native Americans would continue to enjoy a vast superiority of numbers. Indeed, for several years after 1622 it remained a distinct possibility that far from overwhelming the indigenous peoples of the Chesapeake it would be the English themselves who would be overwhelmed.

When the English did capture native Americans, and chose to put them to work on their tobacco fields rather than kill them, the results were far from successful. These captive workers, in a terrain that was quite familiar to them, could easily make their escape back to their own people. Moreover, if the English hoped to retain any credible commercial and trading links with indigenous Americans, it was scarcely good business practice to force some of their number to work against their will. For all these most practical of reasons, Virginia's tobacco producers did not look to native Americans to resolve their labor problems. Another alternative presented itself: the recruitment of a workforce in the Old World. The contemporary English practice of servitude could be modified in ways that would attract English people in sufficient numbers to satisfy Virginia's labor demands.

As with many, if not most, migratory movements, the flow of indentured servants to the Chesapeake reflected a combination of "push" and "pull" factors. The promotional literature that continued to be published in England painted a picture that bore little resemblance to the reality of life for most people in the Virginia of the 1620s and 1630s. But perhaps what mattered most to those in England who were in desperate economic straits, or to those who had a greater ambition than mere economic survival, was what it was that they thought they were being offered in Virginia. True, they would be required to serve for a term of years, usually four or five, in exchange for their passage to America, but, in the shape of their indenture contracts, they were being given what they assumed would be a cast-iron guarantee that at the end of that time they would be able to shed their dependent, servile status. Indentured servitude offered the passport to freedom, the prospect of land ownership, and the possibility of a potentially unlimited upward mobility.

By the mid-1620s indentured servitude had already become a firm fixture in Virginia. In 1625 close to half of the colony's population of just over 1,200 people were described as servants. Their lives as servants did not always conform to their expectations of Virginia or resemble the servile status that many of them had known in England. Their tobacco-producing masters demanded a return on the investment they were making in them. Many sought to secure that return by resorting to the most rigorous physical coercion, especially of those servants who did not work hard, or hard enough, at what were often arduous and unfamiliar agricultural tasks in an unhealthy environment. Some servants absconded and, if they were retaken, could expect to have extra time added on to their term of indenture to compensate their masters for the time they had been absent. Many died during their term of indenture; some who survived found that their masters did not always honor the "freedom dues" itemized in their indenture contracts. But through the middle years of the seventeenth century a high proportion of those who came through their term of indenture could hope to secure land in the Tidewater. What they did with that land, how far they advanced up the economic, social, and political ladder, could not be easily predicted. But allowing for luck and application, there were no predetermined limits to what might be achieved by former servants.

Old World backgrounds and status counted for little in the Virginia of the 1620s and 1630s; it was New World achievements that mattered. A man's status and prestige were determined by the number of acres of land he owned, by the number of pounds of tobacco he was producing. "The Great Chain of Being," a theory that sought to validate the strictly hierarchical ordering of society, did not have the relevance in Virginia that it had for elite sixteenth-century English people or that it would have for eminent Chesapeake planters by the end of the seventeenth century. Nonetheless, in the seventeenth-century Chesapeake colonies the freedom signified by land ownership would not translate into anything approximating economic, social, or political equality.

Indentured servants formed the backbone of Virginia's labor force through the 1680s, and the colony's continuing success in attracting this type of labor from the Old World would be profoundly significant in determining the treatment of another group who were present in Virginia from as early as 1619: West Africans. It is generally held that the first West Africans, twenty of them, were brought to Virginia by a Dutch vessel in August 1619. However, a census taken shortly before Sir George Yeardley arrived from England in April 1619 to take up his post as Governor of Virginia suggests that there were already thirty-two people of African descent in the colony. There appears to be no record of how long they had been in Virginia or of who had taken them there.

For the next half century the African population of the Chesapeake would remain numerically and economically insignificant. In 1625, for example, when another census was taken in Virginia, there were said to be only twenty-three people of African ancestry in the colony. By 1649 that number had increased to about 300 in a total colonial population of around 15,300. Eleven years later it was estimated that around 950 people, or roughly 3.5 percent of Virginia's population of 27,000, were of African descent. In the same year Maryland was home to approximately 758 people of African birth or ancestry, and they accounted for fractionally under 9 percent of the colony's inhabitants.

By 1619 the labor-hungry tobacco planters of Tidewater Virginia knew full well that in other parts of the Americas West Africans had long been seen as the most economically viable workforces for plantation agriculture and, moreover, that they had long since been categorized as slaves by other Europeans— by the Dutch who shipped them across the Atlantic and by the Spanish and Portuguese who purchased and employed them. So why was it that during the 1620s and 1630s, years when they were so desperate for workers, Virginia's tobacco planters failed to emulate the examples being set elsewhere in the New World? There are two possible explanations. First, the profit-motivated tobacco planters of the 1620s and 1630s might have made a shrewd economic calculation that Africans were not, in fact, the most advantageous form of labor available to them. Second, they might have had some ideological antipathy to, or uncertainty about, the institution of slavery and the eligibility of Africans for such a status.

Some historians have sought the failure of Virginia's tobacco planters to make the transition to an African workforce in the 1620s and 1630s in a blend of economic and demographic considerations that were operating on both sides of the Atlantic Ocean. Such an interpretation hinges on the high rates of mortality that were being experienced in Virginia through the 1640s and relies heavily on the assumption that planters believed that West Africans would be as vulnerable as themselves in the epidemiological environment of the Tidewater. English people were still willing to cross to Virginia as indentured servants, and the capital required to secure their services, albeit for a limited term, was significantly less than that needed to purchase an African person who could be made to serve for life, as could their offspring. If the mortality rates of servant and slave were, or were assumed to be, equal, then the economically rational course was to invest in the former rather than in the latter. Ethnicity, the negative stereotyping of West Africans by the English, plays little or no part in this explanation of the behavior of Tidewater planters. They were economically rational men who were driven simply and solely by the profit motive.

That African workers were more expensive to acquire during the 1620s and 1630s than were indentured English servants was certainly the case; that Virginia tobacco producers were profit-driven is indisputable; and that they were economically rational is also well within the bounds of possibility. However, it is important to emphasize that during the 1620s and 1630s, and indeed through the 1680s, Virginia planters were not in a position to make a simple and straightforward choice between European and West African workers. Those Europeans, mainly the Dutch, who were engaged in the transatlantic slave trade during the first half of the seventeenth century had little financial incentive to head for Virginia on anything like a regular basis. The appalling mortality rates of the enslaved Africans who toiled in the plantation economies established by Spain and Portugal in South America and the Caribbean offered a guaranteed market, and good prices, for all the human cargoes they had to sell. There was no compelling reason for slave ships to make the longer journey to what, certainly in the 1620s and 1630s, were considered the less certain markets of the Chesapeake. That longer voyage entailed additional expenses and, given the mortality rates on the Middle Passage, added significantly to the risk of diminishing their anticipated profits.

Perhaps because of their economic rationality, Virginia's tobacco producers did not clamor for African workers during the 1620s and 1630s. Neither did they instantly perceive those twenty Africans who were brought against their will to Virginia by the Dutch in 1619 as being eligible for immediate enslavement by themselves. John Rolfe, one of early Virginia's most eminent settlers, stated quite categorically that these Africans had been "sold" to the colonists by the Dutch, not in the form of a cash transaction but in exchange for provisions. This, however, is something of a technicality. Rather more to the point is precisely what Rolfe might have meant by his use of the word *Sold*, of precisely what commodity it was that the English thought they were buying in the summer of 1619.

Given the manner in which indenture contracts, and thereby the work of English servants, could be bought and sold, it is conceivable that the Virginia settlers believed it was the labor, rather than the persons, of these Africans that they were acquiring. That they thought of these newcomers as being different from themselves is readily apparent from Rolfe's use of the word *Negars* rather than, for example, *servants*. However, it is also significant that Rolfe did not refer to these Africans as being slaves, although this was quite clearly the status that had been bestowed upon them by the Dutch who had brought them to Virginia. Neither did the English immediately devise such a status for them. In fact, through the 1620s and into the 1630s, the African population of the Tidewater Chesapeake, perhaps in part because it remained so small, retained a somewhat ambiguous status in English eyes. Yet some of the seeds of their subsequent enslavement are to be found in this very ambiguity.

By the 1640s, and possibly even earlier, there were some property-owning, and thereby free, people of African ancestry in the Chesapeake. The most well known of them was Anthony Johnson, who had arrived in Virginia in 1621. Thirty years later Johnson claimed, and was granted, a headright of 250 acres of land. Johnson's career provides some of the most potent evidence in support of the argument that the course of race relations in seventeenth-century Virginia was not preordained, that the enslavement of West Africans was by no means a foregone conclusion in the 1620s.

Although the evidence is slender, there is some suggestion that during the 1620s Virginia tobacco planters may have applied exactly the same criteria to the Africans being brought to Virginia as they did to European workers who arrived in the colony without indenture papers. That is to say, they might have been inclined to negotiate either verbal or written terms of employment with them, and those terms could have included promises of freedom that eventually were honored. Anthony Johnson, for example, was specifically referred to in the Virginia census of 1625 as a servant. However, possibly because it was a verbal arrangement, or maybe because any written contract that might have been drawn up did not survive the passage of time, there is no extant record of the agreement reached between Johnson and his master. How many other Africans in the Virginia of the 1620s were in a position to negotiate the terms of their labor, and secured their release from servitude, can never be known. But Johnson's case strongly suggests that this was by no means beyond the realms of possibility; that as yet Virginia's planters had not devised a slave status, a perpetual and heritable servitude, specifically for West Africans.

This is not to say that at least some of the strands of the racial ideology that would enable and encourage this to happen during the second half of the seventeenth century were totally absent from the Virginia of the 1620s and 1630s. Beginning with Rolfe's reference to "Negars," the English in Virginia employed a language that clearly differentiated Africans from themselves. For example, it seems to have been because of their ethnicity rather than because of any distinctive status already assigned to them that Africans were listed separately in the census of 1625. This separate listing may well have carried with it implications of inferiority to the English. However, during the 1620s and 1630s the Virginia colonists did not articulate the differences they perceived between themselves and the Africans in their midst in a language of racial contempt, fear, or hatred.

There is persuasive evidence dating from the 1620s through the 1680s that there were those of European descent in the Chesapeake who were prepared to identify and cooperate with people of African descent. These affinities were forged in the world of plantation work. On many plantations Europeans and West Africans labored side by side in the tobacco fields, performing exactly the same types and amounts of work; they lived and ate together in shared housing; they socialized together; and sometimes they slept together.

Sometimes black and white plantation workers ran away together. A particular episode that took place in 1640, in which six European workers and one African absconded together, is often cited in support of the claim that by this date lifetime service was fast becoming the norm for most Africans in Virginia. When the group was recaptured, the Europeans were made to serve extra time by way of compensating their masters, but the African was branded and made to wear irons. The inference often drawn from this divergence of treatment is that it was already assumed that the latter would serve his master for the rest of his life and therefore the imposition of extra service would have been regarded as a pointless exercise. This incident certainly suggests a drift toward lifetime service, but it is also highly significant for another reason: the cooperation between these men of different ethnic origins.

In the daily world of plantation work, ethnic differences were appreciated by Africans and Europeans alike, but this abortive escape attempt suggests that there could be a mutual willingness to overlook these differences. But as the different punishments meted out to the seven escapees in 1640 suggest, plantation masters were already beginning to differentiate between Africans and Europeans, and they were already beginning to realize that African workers could be more advantageous to them than indentured European servants.

From the planter standpoint, there had always been one serious problem associated with indentured servitude. This system of labor did not provide them with a permanent workforce. Those who survived their term of indenture, and who had the prospect of land ownership, had absolutely no incentive to reenter the labor market as hired hands, and most did not make that choice. They might even go on to compete with their former masters in the labor market; even if they did not, they had to be replaced. The time their masters spent in training them would then have to be spent all over again on their replacements.

Tobacco planters accepted that they were under a legal, and

possibly also a moral, obligation to release English indentured servants at the end of their term of service. During the 1630s it began to dawn on them that they were not necessarily under the same legal obligation to release those Africans who had arrived in Virginia bereft of the guarantees provided by indenture contracts. Moreover, it was these same planters who dominated the courts that arbitrated the contractual relations between masters and their servants. Africans could not expect to find influential allies in Tidewater Virginia, and neither could they hope to find friends in London who would protect their interests. In practice there was nothing to stop those planters who wished to impose lifetime servitude on their African workers from doing precisely that.

By the same token, in practice there was nothing to stop tobacco planters from extending that same lifetime servitude to the children of their African workers. During the 1630s some inventories of estates were beginning to place a higher valuation on African women servants than on their European counterparts. The reasons for this were twofold: an appreciation of the economic value of any children born to African women and the fact that African women could be compelled to work at various agricultural tasks that most European women refused to do. By 1640 two of the main attributes of slavery, a service that was usually for life and could be inherited, with the status of the child following that of its mother, were beginning to emerge as accepted social and economic practices in Tidewater Virginia. They were practices, however, that were not as yet enshrined in law. This was a process that would begin in the 1660s and culminate in 1705 in the passage of a comprehensive slave code for Virginia.

During the 1640s the unmistakable trend toward a lifetime, heritable service for Africans was given an added impetus by events in the Old World. The English Civil War greatly disrupted the flow of migrants to the New World, and the stabilization of wages in the English economy during the postwar decades served to diminish the purely economic reasons for emigration. Moreover, the founding of new colonies by the English (Carolina in the 1660s and Pennsylvania in the 1680s) and the seizure of New Netherland from the Dutch (also in the 1660s) meant that there was heightened colonial competition for a smaller pool of prospective servants. Jamaica also proved an attractive destination for some English migrants who might otherwise have made their way to the mainland. The consequence of all this for the Chesapeake colonies was that English servants were less readily available than had formerly been the case, and as a result they were becoming increasingly expensive to acquire.

Although mortality rates in the Tidewater Chesapeake began to decline during the middle years of the century, tobacco planters remained as desperate as they had always been to obtain a secure and constant supply of workers. They were fast learning to appreciate the economic advantages that stemmed from the employment of Africans. By 1650 or thereabouts many planters were ready to make the switch from indentured to involuntary servitude, and Dutch traders were now eager to help.

Earlier in the century Dutch slave traders had been disinclined to off-load their human cargoes in the Chesapeake. During the 1640s, however, they sought to exploit the disruptions to English shipping caused by England's Civil War in order to secure for themselves a firm commercial foothold in English America. They offered English planters, both in the Caribbean and in the Chesapeake, not only a way of getting their sugar and tobacco to European markets but also an assured supply of workers, African workers. As we shall go on to see, this Dutch connection was to be of paramount importance in the fixing of chattel slavery upon Barbados. In the Chesapeake colonies, the Dutch now saw there not a settlement of a few hundred people struggling against heavy odds to survive but a secure, and potentially limitless, market for all the Africans they could supply. At the same time they were acutely aware of the profits to be made from shipping the Chesapeake's tobacco to the Old World.

The problem for the Dutch and the Chesapeake's tobacco producers, and arguably the main reason why the wholesale switch to African labor was delayed for another twenty years, was fierce English opposition to any and all intrusions by the Dutch into their growing commercial empire. Beginning in 1651, successive English governments enacted legislation, known collectively as the Navigation Acts, that was initially intended to counter the Dutch threat. Partly because the economic needs and aspirations of the English settlers sometimes outweighed their loyalty to the English Crown and Parliament, and partly because they were so difficult to police, the Navigation Acts never completely succeeded in stamping out all Anglo-Dutch connections in the New World. But they did add greatly to the difficulties of those Chesapeake planters who sought African workers and of those traders who were best placed to supply them.

Together with the Navigation Acts, the deteriorating relations between England and Holland that culminated in the Anglo-Dutch Wars of the 1660s and 1670s were to further compound the problems of the Tidewater Chesapeake's tobacco planters. In an attempt to exclude the Dutch from the tobacco trade, the English placed tobacco on the list of enumerated commodities, those that could not be exported directly to continental Europe but had to be reexported through England. It took time for the English merchants who dominated the tobacco trade to organize the reexport trade, and in the meantime the Tidewater economy suffered as tobacco prices fell. But tobacco prices fell during the 1660s and 1670s for another reason that was to have a profound bearing on the transition from indentured European to involuntary African servitude. That reason had to do with the changing demographic and social climate of the Tidewater Chesapeake.

The declining mortality rates of the mid-seventeenth century, and the growth of the Chesapeake's European population through natural increase, greatly exacerbated the difficulties of the region's established tobacco planters. A longer life expectancy meant that now more servants were surviving their term of indenture. Most of those who survived were reluctant, as indentured servants had always been reluctant, to reenter the labor market as hired hands. They wanted their freedom; they wanted land; they wanted to produce tobacco; they wanted to become their own masters and the masters of others. This presented established tobacco planters with a dual problem: securing the workers they needed in the face of this greatly enhanced competition, and securing their socioeconomic standing and political dominance in the face of overproduction of tobacco that could only further depress prices. During the 1660s and 1670s, years when they themselves were embroiled in a bitter power struggle, elite planters devised various means to secure their hegemony. They tried, not always successfully, to extend terms of indenture; they used their political dominance of the House of Burgesses to make it difficult for ex-servants to acquire land, or at least to acquire land cheaply, in the Tidewater; and they even destroyed tobacco crops in an attempt to force up prices.

Yet the fact remained that during these troubled years tobacco planters still required workers. By the 1680s West African workers were being made increasingly available to them,
not now by the Dutch but by English merchants and shippers
who were keenly appreciative of the profits to be made from
the transatlantic slave trade. The organization of the Royal African Company in 1672 offered planters the prospect of a
steady supply of the workers they required at prices that made
them increasingly competitive with the dwindling number of
indentured servants now arriving in the Chesapeake, and it was
an opportunity the planters grasped with alacrity. The willingness of English merchants to extend credit to those elite tobacco planters who needed it in order to acquire laborers
would greatly facilitate the transition to a predominantly African agricultural workforce.

The speed with which the Chesapeake's eminent tobacco
planters completely transformed the region's labor base, and
thereby its racial composition, after 1680 bears some comparison with the situation in Barbados. In 1680 there were roughly
4,000 people of African descent in Virginia and Maryland, the
vast majority of them in the Tidewater counties. Thirty years
later, there were around 23,100 persons of African birth or
descent in Virginia (about 42 percent of the colony's total population), and in Maryland 8,000 Africans accounted for 23 percent of that colony's inhabitants. In neither colony was there
any longer any significant ambiguity about the Africans' status.
By 1710 a racially based system of chattel slavery was firmly
fixed. Virginia and Maryland had been transformed from
slaveholding societies into slave societies.

Thus, during the middle years of the seventeenth century
elite tobacco planters increasingly assumed the right to do as
they pleased with their African workers. That assumption was

legally sanctioned in 1669. In that year the eminent planters who dominated the House of Burgesses considered the question of what punishments they could legitimately inflict on their African workers. Indicative of the punishments that were already being meted out by some of their number, they debated the legal standing of masters who killed their workers "by the extremity of the correction" they inflicted. Were such masters liable to stand trial for murder? The Burgesses agreed that they were not, because "it cannot be presumed that prepensed malice (which alone makes murther [sic] Felony) should induce any man to destroy his own estate." Two things remained to be determined: what rights, if any, would be retained by those who were now being defined as the "estate" of their masters, and were there any grounds upon which Africans could legitimately claim their release from the bondage being devised for them?

The planters of Virginia were aware of the long tradition of English thinking on the relationship between Christianity and bondage, but they had their own pragmatic interpretation of this tradition. Could one Christian hold another Christian in bondage? Did a slave's conversion to Christianity constitute an irrefutable argument for the freeing of that slave? What prompted the Virginian discourses on this subject during the 1660s and 1670s is not altogether clear. There were some Africans in the Tidewater who embraced Christianity, and who perhaps were already beginning to see in Christian theology a possible escape route from the slavery being forced on them. It is also possible that elite planters were anticipating what they incorrectly believed might be English objections to the status they were devising for the Africans in their midst. If nothing else, though, they did not want to concede to those Africans any wedge, any conceivable bargaining power, that might derive from a common religion. In laws drafted in the 1660s and 1670s, Virginia planters declared quite unambiguously, as much to Africans as to anyone else, that as far as they were concerned Christianity and bondage were perfectly compatible. At the same time, and something that would continue through the era of the American Revolution, most planters discouraged any and all attempts on the part of churchmen to convert their bond-people.

The planters' position, which was exactly the same as that of the Barbadian sugar planters, could be justified only by recourse to familiar stereotypes. Africans had to be depicted as being both unwilling and unable to embrace Christianity; if necessary, their very humanity had to be denied.

The slave status defined in the Chesapeake owed something to long-standing abstract English concepts of slavery; increasingly, though, it would be infused with a language of racial hatred that sought to debase and to dehumanize those of African descent. This explicitly racist language was employed quite deliberately by men who had a vested interest in the enslavement of Africans. Some, perhaps, felt the need to salve their consciences. Others, and possibly the majority, might have anticipated that such language, together with the harsh physical treatment of Africans that they were legally sanctioning, would serve another desirable purpose.

Elite planters had every reason to try to enlist the support of nonelite whites, to nullify the mutually supportive links that the letter had forged and might continue to forge with people of African descent. What eminent planters required were compliant nonelite whites who would help them police their African workers. The planters thus used racist language to develop their own alliance with the nonelite whites, one based purely on skin color.

Following on the sixteenth-century practice, the early colonists had commonly referred to themselves as "Christians" and
to native Americans and West Africans as "Heathens." It was
not a matter of chance that during the second half of the seventeenth century this terminology began to change to one of
"White" and "Black." At the end of the seventeenth century it
still remained to be seen whether the white alliance envisaged
by elite planters, with all that it was likely to entail for the
future, would be effected. From the planters' perspective, however, the omens looked promising. On the one hand, the switch
to a predominantly African agricultural workforce greatly diminished opportunities for fraternization in the workplace.
Nonelite whites may have lived in the midst of the Chesapeake's growing African population, but, in a very profound
sense, they became spatially separated from that population.

During the second half of the seventeenth century, and principally because of the steps taken by elite planters to secure
their hegemony, the opportunities available to indentured servants in the Tidewater Chesapeake to achieve the freedom, the
upward social, economic, and political mobility that had lured
so many of them across the Atlantic, diminished dramatically.
After 1650 probably no more than about 6 percent of indentured servants went on to become independent planters in the
Tidewater. Most of the ex-servants who remained there found
that through tenancy or by reentering the labor market as hired
hands they were tied to an economic, social, and political regime over which they exercised little, if any, control. But this
did not necessarily mean that they ceased to aspire to land
ownership. Some turned their backs on the Chesapeake in the
hope of realizing their ambitions elsewhere in the mainland.
Few of those who remained in the Tidewater could have been
in any doubt that the one sure way to freedom and to wealth,

the ownership of land and of enslaved people to work that land, was fast becoming way beyond their reach. None seriously doubted that in the context of the Tidewater's agricultural economy African slaves were proving far more profitable workers than any others who were currently available.

Not all nonelite whites in the Chesapeake had necessarily been persuaded by the racist rhetoric and practices of elite planters, or saw a planter lifestyle that they particularly admired and wished to emulate. But even so, they must have found it difficult to identify with, and in the short term even to communicate with, the African-born peoples who were being shipped to the Chesapeake in ever-increasing numbers after 1680. By the same token, there was no compelling reason why African women and men who had been torn from their families and friends, who had been made to endure the horrors of the Middle Passage to America, should have elected to make common cause with any European person.

In 1705, almost exactly a century after the first colonists had set foot in Jamestown, the House of Burgesses codified and systematized Virginia's laws of slavery. These laws would be modified and added to over the next century and a half, but the essential legal framework within which the institution of slavery would subsequently operate had been put in place. It had taken the English in Virginia the best part of one hundred years to finalize their construction of a legal status quite unknown in the Common Law of England, to declare unequivocally that Africans were a form of property; that they were, and henceforth would remain, "strangers" and "outsiders" who would be required to live out their lives according to an entirely different set of laws from those that governed people of European birth and ancestry.

The process of enslavement in the seventeenth-century

Chesapeake colonies might appear to have been slow and so it was, but only in comparison with the speed with which West Africans were enslaved by the English in the Caribbean. For essentially practical, rather than for any theoretical or moral, reasons, it took those who settled in Virginia far longer than those who made for the Caribbean to design a slave status specifically for West Africans. But those English people who settled in the Caribbean and the southern mainland during the first half of the seventeenth century were by no means alone in originating a legal status that was unknown in the Common Law of England. In New England, too, the English settlers would devise a slave status, but it was one that would not necessarily be confined to those of West African ancestry.

5

"Godly Society":
Slavery Among Puritans
and Quakers

In 1660, when enslaved Africans accounted for just over one-half of the Barbadian population, New England's total population numbered just under 33,000 and included only 560 people of West African ancestry. Half a century later, mainly because of natural increase rather than because of continuing immigration to the region, the New England population had more than tripled in size to around 111,800. The African component of this population had increased in absolute terms, but not relative to the number of Europeans.

The 1,885 Africans said to be in the New England colonies in 1710 still accounted for less than 2 percent of the region's total population. Massachusetts contained the largest number of Africans, approximately 1,310 out of a total population of 61,080, and Rhode Island, with around 5 percent, the highest proportion of Africans in its population. To put this proportion into some kind of perspective, the roughly 375 people it represented was equivalent to the number that might be imported to any of England's plantation colonies on a single slave ship. These figures might seem to suggest that slavery was of little consequence in and for seventeenth-century New England.

There is an element of truth in such a view, but only if the New England experience is set against those of the plantation colonies of the English Caribbean and southern mainland.

At no point in the seventeenth century were West Africans essential to the successful functioning of the New England economy. In fact, it was the character of that economy, rather than the social, ethnic, religious, and racial imperatives of the Puritans, that militated against the employment of African workers on a scale comparable with that of the plantation colonies. Of all the English people who set out to colonize the New World during the first half of the seventeenth century, however, it was the Puritans who had the most clearly defined images of freedom and bondage. Those images raised the distinct possibility that they would resort to some form of bondage in the Americas, regardless of the environment in which they settled.

In 1641, within a decade of the arrival of the first settlers in Massachusetts Bay, the Puritans drafted their Body of Liberties, a document in which they legally sanctioned the existence of bondage in their "Godly Society." The arguments they marshaled to justify such a step implied that under certain circumstances the status of bond servant might be conferred on Europeans, including some English people. However, the practice of bondage in seventeenth-century New England would involve the enslavement not of Europeans, or of other English people, but of native Americans and those of West African descent. In this respect New England's slave system would bear more than a passing resemblance to those that developed elsewhere in English America. In other respects, though, and not simply in its demographic, economic, and ethnic dimensions, it would be profoundly different from these other systems.

The distinctive Puritan concept of bondage derived from a

particular blend of social, political, and, perhaps above all else, religious thought that informed their "Errand into the Wilderness." The Puritan practice of slavery would also be informed by a cluster of ethnic images and stereotypes that they held in common with other English colonists in the New World. That the Puritan concept of slavery would retain much of its integrity when translated into practice owed much to the particular American environment in which John Winthrop and his associates sought to establish their "City upon a Hill."

The original Puritan design for the Godly Society they intended to build in the New World was infused with sixteenth- and early-seventeenth-century elite English thinking about social hierarchy, order, and orderliness. John Winthrop, after all, was a member of the Suffolk gentry and he subscribed to all the social and political imperatives of that class. That Winthrop should have attached the importance he did to the elite ideal of the immutability of social rank, to the gentry desire for social rigidity and, therefore, social stability, is scarcely surprising. Under his leadership the society established by the Puritans in Massachusetts would enshrine and perpetuate these ideals and qualities. But, of course, that society would also reflect something else: the burning desire of the Puritans to create a community in which the will of God would be observed in every detail. Quite literally, Winthrop and his group set out to establish God's kingdom on earth.

Central to this intent was the belief that every nation or people—and the Puritans believed that they were God's chosen people—existed by virtue of a covenant, or a contract, made with God. The Puritans were convinced that if they kept to their side of the agreement, if they lived according to God's laws, then they could expect divine protection. Their interpretation of God's laws, as set out in their reading of the Bible, established the parameters of acceptance in Winthrop's City upon a Hill, of Puritan exclusivity, at the same time as it reinforced elite English notions of hierarchy, of order, of stability.

The covenanted theology of the Puritans distinguished between three covenants: the covenant of grace, or the invisible church of saints; the church covenant, or the visible church on earth; and the civil covenant that would form the basis of government in Massachusetts. Puritan exclusivity was such that not everyone was eligible to become a member of the church covenant. In order to be accepted into the church, individuals had to make a public declaration that they had experienced a sense of their own salvation and provide convincing evidence that they had lived a blameless life. Not least because of the secular privileges it conferred, church membership was highly desirable. In Massachusetts, political participation, political freedom would be tied not to land ownership but to church membership.

Individuals who were accepted into church membership had voluntarily entered into a covenant, or contract, with their fellow church members in much the same way as the Puritans as a whole believed that they had entered into a covenant with God. The spiritual equality implicit in church membership, however, did not carry over into secular life. Social equality was not a Puritan ideal—quite the contrary, in fact. The social structure Winthrop envisaged for Massachusetts was that of a rigid hierarchy predicated on the notion of a divine calling. The individual's occupation, and thereby social rank, was divinely determined and irrevocably fixed and irrelevant to salvation. What mattered to God, the Puritans insisted, was the diligence with which individuals pursued their divine calling, however humble that calling might be. The earthly rewards offered by God for such diligence did not include the promise of upward social mobility, either to members of the present generation or to their children.

Winthrop's design, then, was based on the assumption that there were those who were born to wealth, to social and political eminence, and those who were not. Similarly, there were those who were born to be served and those who were born to serve. Initially it was assumed by the Puritan leaders that familiar, traditional English patterns of service, of contractual employment, would suffice to meet the economic requirements of Massachusetts. In 1641, as part of a broader attempt to define the character and operation of their Godly Society, to define their own particular brand of Englishness, and to justify steps that they had already taken, the Puritans stated quite categorically that another form of servitude might legitimately exist in Massachusetts. The theoretical justification for this form of bondage was deeply rooted in abstract English concepts of slavery and freedom. Its practical implementation, already under way by 1641, would be just as deeply rooted in late-sixteenth- and early-seventeenth-century English ethnocentricity.

Like those English people who had preceded them to the Tidewater Chesapeake, the first Puritan migrants were forced to contemplate the nature of their relationship with the indigenous peoples of New England. Puritan impressions of, and intentions for, native Americans incorporated the same ambiguity, the same negative and positive images, that had long permeated English thinking. On the one hand, they believed that native Americans were capable of being "civilized" and that they would warmly embrace the Puritan version of English civilization. Indeed, the proselytization of those whom they sometimes described as "barbarous heathens" was seen as a divinely ordained aim of the Puritans' Errand into the Wilderness. That proselytization, however, would be on terms dictated by the Puritans and, moreover, would not entail the complete acceptance of indigenous Americans into their exclusive Godly Society.

As was the case with other English colonizers, the Puritans also expected that the indigenous peoples of New England would form invaluable trading partners. Unlike many of the English migrants who made for the Tidewater Chesapeake and the eastern Caribbean during the first third of the seventeenth century, the Puritans who crossed the Atlantic in the 1630s did not do so with the explicit intention of securing enormous individual fortunes. Neither did they intend simply to scratch out a subsistence standard of living in the New World. Provided it could be achieved in ways that conformed to Winthrop's edict that "the care of the public must oversway all private respects," the Puritans had no serious objections to the making of money. It was not money, or wealth per se, that lay at the root of all evil but the love of money, the unacceptable personal motives and behavior that might be associated with the making of money and the stewardship of wealth. From the outset, the Puritans knew also that through the fur trade or through other commercial connections, indigenous Americans would play a significant role in defining their standard of living.

There were, then, positive aspects of the Puritan stereotyping of native Americans, both pragmatic and ideological, but they were held in tandem with other, far more negative images and expectations. Thus, if only for pragmatic reasons, the first Puritan migrants could take the recent diphtheria epidemic that had devastated the indigenous peoples of the Massachusetts Bay region as a sign of God's blessing on their project. Within three or four years of establishing their first settlement at Boston they could interpret the behavior of native Americans in a

manner that reinforced their image of a "barbarous," "uncivilized" people. These people were not only rejecting English
civilization but doing so in a manner that threatened the very
existence of the Puritans' Godly Society. In Massachusetts, as
in the Tidewater Chesapeake, it would be land that brought
the negative English stereotypes of indigenous Americans to
the fore.

John Winthrop had intended that the first Puritan migrants
would settle together in one community, one township, but the
desire of those migrants for local autonomy, one of their main
reasons for leaving England, meant that this was not to be. The
availability of land offered groups of migrants from particular
English localities the prospect of establishing their own essentially self-regulating, self-governing townships, and Winthrop
was unable to prevent them from doing so. By 1640 the continuing stream of Puritan migrants had formed over fifteen
such townships, and herein lay the origins of the rapidly deteriorating relations between these migrants and the indigenous
peoples of New England.

Initially, the territorial encroachments made by the Puritans
were of a very different order from those associated with tobacco cultivation farther south. The heavy flow of migrants to
Massachusetts during the 1630s, however, and the rapid growth
of that population thereafter would mean the continual expansion of settlement. With the notable exception of Roger Wil-
liams, who soon fell out with Winthrop and left Massachusetts
to create his own vision of a Godly Society in Rhode Island,
most Puritans had no misgivings about simply taking the land
they needed for their townships. They appreciated, could not
help but appreciate, that the land they sought was already occupied, but did the indigenous occupants have any right to the
land?

To begin with, the settlers of Massachusetts fervently hoped that they could coexist harmoniously with the indigenous peoples of New England. But they reserved the right to defend themselves, and thereby the lands upon which they had settled, should that ever prove necessary. They also believed that, without necessarily waging war in order to secure them, they had every right to occupy lands that they described as "the Lord's Waste." Native Americans had been accorded custody of the land by God, the Puritans argued, but they had not "minded the employment thereof to the right ends for which the land was created." That is to say, they had not introduced European-style agricultural economies, and, equally delinquent of them, neither had they initiated property rights that were in keeping with European models. On both these counts, the Puritans insisted, native Americans could be said to have forfeited their right to the land they occupied.

The founding of townships by the early settlers of Massachusetts, and by 1633 the expansion of settlement into the fertile lands of the Connecticut River valley, brought the Puritans into direct conflict with the Pequot and Narraganset peoples. Compared with the territorial encroachments of the tobacco-producing planters, those made by the New England settlers were modest in the extreme. But they were large enough, and persistent enough, to persuade the Pequots and Narragansets that at all costs they must be resisted.

In 1633 and 1634 some English traders were murdered, or so it was alleged, by the Pequots. Eleven years earlier in Virginia the so-called Massacre of 1622 had provided the English settlers there with the excuse they needed to wage all-out war in order to secure land. Precisely the same thing happened in New England following the death of these English traders. This was the justification the Puritans needed, or felt they needed, to launch a punitive attack on the Pequots. A force of around one hundred men was dispatched from Massachusetts to the Connecticut River valley to exact revenge. But the Pequots, in alliance with the Narragansets, proved a formidable enemy, and in 1635 and 1636 they devastated the English settlements of Saybrook and Wethersfield.

The Puritan response was harsh and uncompromising: Pequot villages were attacked and destroyed; men, women, and children were put to the sword. But what of those who were not? What would be the fate of those whose lives had been spared by their Puritan captors? The answer arrived at by the Puritans was firmly rooted in traditional English thought. These ungrateful "heathen" peoples, the Puritans insisted, had been captured in a war that fitted the description of a just war. As such, they might be legitimately enslaved. However, their continuing presence as captive slaves in the Puritan settlements could not be guaranteed—they might escape from their Puritan captors with comparative ease and rejoin their compatriots. Moreover, their enslavement might provoke potentially devastating reprisals. The Puritan solution, to help safeguard their own security rather than because of moral qualms, was to remove these native American captives as far away from themselves as possible. The English settlements in the Caribbean, and particularly the Puritan presence on St. Kitts and, between 1630 and 1641, on Providence Island, offered the New England Puritans an ideal solution to their problem. The native American captives could be shipped there, where they would be compelled to labor for the English settlers.

That such an arrangement was practically possible reflected what, by the late 1630s, was beginning to emerge as an increasingly important, if still a somewhat contentious, sector of the Massachusetts economy: overseas trade. The first settlers of

Massachusetts encountered a physical environment that, although different, was not unrecognizably different from that which they had known in the Old World. On the one hand, this facilitated the introduction of familiar crops and agricultural practices. On the other hand, the soils and climate of New England militated against the production of lucrative staple crops and, in the process, helped to safeguard the integrity of the tightly knit townships that were so profoundly important to the Puritans.

By the late 1630s the Puritan settlers were growing enough basic foodstuffs to support themselves and, while it proved necessary, also to feed those who were following them across the Atlantic to Massachusetts. In addition, the rich fishing banks off the New England coast were there to be exploited, and, together with furs, fish provided a potentially valuable commodity for sale in Old World markets. But the Puritan settlements in the Caribbean provided another market for surpluses of grain, meat, fish, and, increasingly, timber. By 1640 these markets were being exploited by merchants based in Boston and the other, smaller port towns that were starting to spring up along the New England coast. It was to be as a direct result of these early trading connections that the first people of African descent were brought from the Caribbean to Massachusetts, probably in 1638 and apparently in exchange for the captives taken in the Pequot War.

In 1641, in order to justify their past and possibly future treatment of indigenous Americans if only to themselves, the Puritans formally and publicly articulated their concept of bondage. It was a concept that established the grounds upon which those Africans already in Massachusetts, and those who might subsequently be taken there, might be legitimately enslaved. However, the Puritans' main objective in 1641, as the

Civil War was getting underway in England, was to elaborate and to assert their own rights and liberties, their own understanding of what it meant to be a "freeborn" Englishman; of who could, and who could not, qualify for this status and all the benefits and blessings that it bestowed. This was the essence of the Body of Liberties, a written statement of the rights and liberties claimed by the Puritans; a document that also stipulated the circumstances under which individual rights and liberties could be forfeited.

The Puritans justified bondage on grounds that would have been entirely familiar to sixteenth-century English and continental European theorists. According to the Body of Liberties, those liable for enslavement in Massachusetts were "lawful captives, taken in just wars, and such strangers as willingly sell themselves, or are sold to us." Theoretically, the word *strangers* could be interpreted as embracing anyone, of any nationality or religion whatsoever, who did not fit the exclusive identity the Puritans had constructed for themselves. In practice, for the purposes of the bondage they envisaged, the Puritan definition of *strangers* would conform to an equally familiar English model: native Americans and people of West African descent were made to fit that description in a way that others were not.

English migrants who did not subscribe to the Puritanism of John Winthrop and his followers, the Baptists and Quakers who made their way to Massachusetts in the mid-seventeenth century, were strangers who were imprisoned, beaten, and sometimes even executed for their beliefs. But no doubt because of the protection afforded by their nationality, and perhaps because of the belief that these errant Protestants might be persuaded of the error of their religious ways, they were never enslaved by the Puritans. From the outset the practice of bondage in Massachusetts would be predicated upon ethnicity.

In a society that had been founded with a view to implementing divine law, it was scarcely surprising that the Puritans should have looked to the Bible for guidance about the practice, as well as about the theory, of bondage. Having outlined the circumstances under which an individual might qualify for bondage, the Body of Liberties went on to insist that "such shall have the liberties and Christian usage which the Law of God established in Israel concerning such persons doth morally require."

The implications of this assertion were twofold. First, using the Old Testament as their guide, the Puritans were applying their interpretation of the Judaic model of servitude to their own situation. In effect, this meant that in Massachusetts bond servants, or slaves, would fall somewhere between the Jewish servant and the gentile slave, somewhere between the indentured servant and the chattel slave. They would be legally defined as pieces of property over which their owners held rights, but they would also retain their legal existence as persons. In the latter capacity they would continue to enjoy a range of rights, and a degree of protection, denied by other English colonists to those whom they enslaved. At least in theory, bond servants in Massachusetts would be permitted to sue and to be sued in the courts; they would enjoy the right to trial by jury; they would be entitled to hold property in their own right. In a society that placed such an emphasis on the universality of justice, bond servants had some expectation of being able to exercise and to maintain these rights.

The second important implication of the Body of Liberties for the practice of bondage in Massachusetts had to do with the demand that bond servants receive "Christian usage" from their owners. Here the Puritans were addressing a point that the Anglican slave owners of the plantation colonies simply rejected out of hand: their obligations as Christian masters and mistresses. Like the Anglicans, the Puritans saw no inconsistency whatsoever between bondage and Christianity. On the contrary, they held that bondage was divinely sanctioned. However, they took the position in 1641 that Christian masters and mistresses had a dual responsibility toward their servants and slaves, to those who were dependent upon them. They must attend not only to the physical welfare of their charges but also to their spiritual well-being. In the case of their Christian servants and slaves this meant ensuring that their behavior conformed to the standards demanded by Christian morality; in the case of their non-Christian dependents it meant introducing them to Christianity and, if possible, helping to secure their conversion. As far as Africans were concerned, the implication was clear enough: they were perfectly capable of understanding the fundamental tenets of Christian teaching, and it was up to their masters, as well as the clergy, to ensure that they did so. In what was to prove a striking contrast with the situation that developed in each of England's plantation colonies, at no point did the Puritans seek to deny the very humanity of West Africans.

Increasingly after 1641 it was West Africans, rather than indigenous Americans, who were forced to fit the Puritan definition of slavery and servitude. The surviving evidence suggests that through the remainder of the seventeenth century, and indeed for the remainder of the colonial period, people of African descent in Massachusetts continued to enjoy many of the rights enshrined in the Body of Liberties. In the realm of both civil and criminal law they continued to receive something approximating an equality of judicial treatment. They never lost the right to sue on their own behalf, and, during the era of the American Revolution, they would be able to employ this right to sue in the courts, and petition the government of Massachusetts, for their complete freedom from slavery. Such a possibility had never been, and never would be, open to the enslaved populations of the plantation colonies.

It is invidious to suggest that any one English American slave system was better than any other for those forced to endure it. This is, however, a case that is often made for Massachusetts. It is true that the enslaved people of that colony retained the legal as well as the social recognition of their humanity, and a number of vitally important legal and personal rights that went along with that recognition. It is, also undeniable that their working lives, although hard, were not as brutally hard as those of their compatriots in the plantation colonies. Moreover, bondpeople in seventeenth-century Massachusetts were generally better clothed, better fed, and better housed than were those in the English Caribbean and southern mainland. On the other hand, they were exposed to an infinitely greater degree of spiritual and cultural coercion than were enslaved West Africans in the plantation colonies. This form of coercion, together with a more benign physical treatment, may well have reflected the religiously infused Puritan ideology of bondage. But it was almost certainly indicative of something else as well: the comparatively small number of enslaved people in Massachusetts.

Unlike the planters of Tidewater Virginia and Barbados, the New England colonists had no reason to feel that they were under intense physical or cultural threat from the enslaved component of their population. There were comparatively few people of African ancestry in the region and, outside the port towns, they were widely dispersed. True, there was always the possibility of violent acts being perpetrated by individual slaves, or by small groups of bondpeople, but an uprising on the scale of those experienced in Barbados and Jamaica during the 1670s was not even remotely possible. If the New Englanders did consider themselves to be under serious physical and cultural assault, it was from the indigenous peoples of the region. Of course, it might have been another story entirely had New England's labor needs been different.

In 1645 Emmanuel Downing wrote to John Winthrop, his brother-in-law, hoping for "a stock of slaves sufficient to do all our business," and it is evident from the tone of his letter that he was thinking in terms of enslaved African workers. It is indisputable that the economic development of seventeenth-century Massachusetts reflected a willingness to exploit people of West African descent. From the 1630s onward, New England merchants had no compunction in shipping goods produced by African workers elsewhere in the Americas. By the late seventeenth century the sugar and sugar products brought from the West Indies formed the basis of a thriving rum industry in New England. Neither did New England traders have any qualms about shipping enslaved West Africans from one part of English America to another or about trying to secure for themselves a foothold in the lucrative transatlantic slave trade. Furthermore, they were perfectly willing to dispose of whatever African workers they could in the port towns of New England to prospective employers who were equally willing to acquire them. The fact of the matter, though, was that neither the urban nor the rural economies of seventeenth-century New England demanded a continuing inflow of workers on a scale, or of a type, comparable with the plantation colonies. The small, mixed family farms that, from the outset, characterized seventeenth-century New England's agricultural economy created little demand for more labor than could be supplied by the family, perhaps with the assistance of a few extra hands at particularly busy times of the farming year.

Moreover, at no point in the seventeenth century was New England hit by the kind of mortality rates that might have created a compelling demand for additional labor of any sort. At a comparatively early date the New England population began to reproduce itself on a scale that amply satisfied the labor requirements of both the rural and urban sectors of the region's economy. True, there were niches in both sectors that came to be filled by enslaved African workers, but outside the port towns these workers were comparatively few and far between.

People of African descent were present in relatively small numbers in New England from the late 1630s onward, and, during the remainder of the century, they would perform many different kinds of work. However, the pattern of slaveholding in seventeenth-century New England was utterly different from that which came to characterize the plantation colonies. Only a minuscule proportion of New Englanders owned slaves, and they were never in a position to impose their will on the majority. Most owners held only one or two slaves and very often they worked alongside them in the fields, on fishing and trading boats, or in workshops. This close proximity, the familiarity it must have engendered, may well have accounted for the comparatively milder physical treatment of enslaved people in New England. It might also have encouraged some masters to think of their slaves in a very traditional English manner: as members, albeit subservient members, of their household. Puritan ideology too—the obligations of Christian masters and mistresses toward their dependents—also fostered attitudes and behavior that would have been unthinkable to the vast majority of slave owners in the plantation colonies. It is difficult to imagine a seventeenth-century Barbadian sugar planter saying, as did Cotton Mather, that his slaves were "in some sense my children."

By the end of the seventeenth century most New England colonists would have agreed with Mather that these "children" could never attain adulthood, could never be placed on a par with themselves. "Children" they might remain, but ought they to remain as enslaved children? Seventeenth-century New Englanders discoursed endlessly about their own rights and liberties, about their Englishness, but after 1641 they had comparatively little to say about the legitimacy of bondage or the racial dimensions of their slave system. Not until the first decade of the eighteenth century would they be called upon by one of their number, Judge Samuel Sewall of Boston, to justify their continuing enslavement of West Africans and their growing participation in the transatlantic slave trade.

Sewall anticipated many of the religious arguments that would be employed by the critics of slavery during the era of the American Revolution, but his stinging critique of slavery and the slave trade provoked virtually no response. The only person who put pen to paper in an attempt to refute Sewall's antislavery arguments, a merchant named John Saffin, reiterated what to his readers would have been entirely familiar biblical justifications for bondage. But he also added something else with which no doubt many of his readers would have sympathized: the argument that, by nature, West Africans were eligible candidates for enslavement. In a language that harked back to sixteenth-century English accounts of West Africa and its inhabitants, Saffin asserted that West Africans were innately "Cowardly and Cruel," "Libidinous, Deceitful, False, and Rude," and "Prone to Revenge." They were "heathens," they were "savages," who could quite legitimately be enslaved by the Christian, "civilized" English colonists.

The exchange between Sewall and Saffin has been of greater interest to historians than it apparently was to their contemporaries. It did not mark the beginning of a sustained debate in the New England colonies on the institution of slavery; it did not signal the beginning of an antislavery movement in the region. As of 1700 slavery and the continuing enslavement of Africans was a generally accepted, and noncontroversial, aspect of life in New England. Precisely the same was true of England's Middle Atlantic colonies of Pennsylvania and New York.

In a purely spatial sense, the origins of Pennsylvania and New York are to be found in the military resolution of the Anglo-Dutch commercial rivalry that had been so crucially important through the middle years of the seventeenth century. From the English perspective, one of the most significant outcomes of the Anglo-Dutch wars of the 1660s and 1670s was the seizure of the vast territories that made up the Dutch colony of New Netherland. That colony, with its superb natural harbor of New Amsterdam, dated back to the 1620s, and, in the decades that followed, it was used by the Dutch West India Company as a base for its commercial operations in the New World.

Partly as an offshoot of its slave-trading activities, and partly to meet the labor requirements of the Dutch settlers who carved out large estates in the Hudson River Valley, the Dutch West India Company had brought West Africans to New Netherland as early as 1628. By 1660, on the eve of its acquisition by the English, New Netherland's population of roughly 5,000 included around 600 enslaved Africans. In absolute terms, the number of Africans was similar to that of Massachusetts; in relative terms, the proportion of Africans was closer to that of Virginia.

The Articles of Capitulation agreed to by the Dutch in 1664 were comparatively generous. Those Dutch settlers who wished to leave the colony were given eighteen months in which to do so; those who chose to remain would be required to take an oath of loyalty to the English Crown and thereafter would be considered free inhabitants under English law. They would be granted liberty of religious conscience and allowed to continue their own customs concerning inheritance. They were also assured of their continuing property rights, including the right to hold slaves.

There was never any question of the English trying to dismantle the slave system that already existed in New York, as they renamed the colony in honor of the King's younger brother, James, Duke of York. On the contrary, in 1665 the continuance of that slave system was sanctioned by the New York Assembly. Significantly, that Assembly was dominated by Puritans who had migrated from New England to Long Island, bringing with them their own distinctive views concerning the legitimacy of slavery. But during the last two decades of the seventeenth century, chattel slavery would become of much greater economic and demographic significance in New York than it ever had been, or ever would be, in New England.

The slave-trading activities begun by the Dutch continued after the English occupation, and, like their counterparts elsewhere in the northern mainland, New York's merchants and shippers were by no means reluctant to satisfy the local demand for workers. Enslaved Africans were put to work, as they had long been put to work, in both the rural and the urban sectors of the New York economy. The often-huge estates of the Hudson Valley, with their proportionately larger labor requirements, offered a market for enslaved workers as did the shipping and ancillary manufacturing industries associated with the port of New York. The number, and proportion, of Africans in the colonial population as a whole grew steadily but, compared with the plantation colonies, not dramatically. By 1710,

New York's population of just over 18,800 included around 2,800 people of African descent. In both absolute and relative terms, however, there were more Africans in New York than there were in any other northern colony.

During the 1660s and 1670s it remained to be seen whether the institution of slavery would be introduced to those parts of New Amsterdam given away to some of his friends by the Duke of York and, if so, what form that slavery would take. Two men, Governor William Berkeley and Sir George Carteret, both of whom were actively involved in the founding of Carolina, were the main beneficiaries of the Duke of York's largesse. They received enormous land grants to the south and southwest of the Hudson Valley, a vast territory that eventually would be carved up into the colonies of New Jersey, Delaware, and Pennsylvania. During the 1670s Berkeley sold his share in New Jersey to two English Quakers, John Fenwick and Edward Byllynge, and this was to mark the beginnings of Quaker attempts to form colonies of their own in the New World.

By the mid-1670s English Quakers, and most famously William Penn, were toying with the idea of establishing a settlement in the New World that would serve, at least in part, as a religious sanctuary. However, those concerned also hoped to make money out of such a colony. When Fenwick and Byllynge fell out, and Penn was called in to arbitrate, the opportunity to establish a Quaker colony presented itself. In 1676, after complicated and protracted negotiations, a consortium headed by Penn was able to take control of West New Jersey, while Carteret retained his interest in East New Jersey. Upon Carteret's death in 1681 a group of twelve Quakers purchased East New Jersey for the princely sum of £3,400.

William Penn was actively involved in planning the Quaker settlement of New Jersey, but by 1680 he was keen to establish a colony of his own on the North American mainland. That he was able to do so owed much to his relationship with the King, who, in 1681, granted him rights as the sole proprietor of a vast territory between the Delaware River and the northern boundary of Maryland. The plan of settlement and form of government devised for this new colony of Pennsylvania were the work of one man, William Penn.

It is often said that William Penn's Quakerism, and not least the notions of spiritual equality and pacifism that it entailed, prompted what by the standards of the times was an enlightened policy toward the indigenous peoples of the Delaware Valley. There is certainly some truth in this assessment, although, in keeping with previous colonial proprietors, Penn had pragmatic reasons for wishing to maintain a working relationship with those whose lands he was seeking to take for his "Holy Experiment."

One might also have thought that there were elements within Quakerism that would militate against the enslavement of Africans in Pennsylvania and Quaker involvement in the transatlantic slave trade. After all, in 1676 George Fox, the founder of the Society of Friends, had issued a clarion call to those Quakers who had settled in Barbados and who had chosen to become slave owners. They would do well to remember, he insisted, "that *Christ* died for all, both *Turks, Barbarians, Tartarians*, and *Ethiopians*; he died for the *Tawnies* and for the *Blacks*, as well as for you that are called *whites*." Here was a bold assertion of the spiritual equality of West Africans, but Fox went even further than this. Unlike Puritan thinkers, he interpreted the pattern of bondage set out in the Old Testament in a manner that demanded the eventual freedom of bond servants. Significantly, he focused on the Jewish servant rather than on the gentile slave. Fox did not mince his words:

those Quakers who held "*Negroes* and *Blacks*, whom they have bought with their Money, [should] let them go free after a considerable Term of Years, if they have served them faithfully." Here Fox was anticipating eighteenth-century antislavery notions of gradual emancipation. But he demanded something more for former slaves in addition to their unconditional release from bondage: "when they go, and are made free, *let them not go away empty handed.*" In the Fox scheme of things, former slaves should receive material compensation for their term of bondage.

The Quaker slave owners of Barbados remained unconvinced by Fox's exhortation. Most saw no inconsistency between their brand of Christianity and the holding of slaves, or any good reason why they should release their slaves, even "after a considerable Term of Years." What they did accept though, something that resulted in their brutal repression by the planter-dominated government of Barbados, was that they had a responsibility to proselytize their African workers. Whether they wished for it or not, bondpeople held by Quaker owners in Barbados were more than likely to receive religious instruction.

The physical contexts of Pennsylvania and Barbados could scarcely have been more different, but the attitudes of their Quaker residents toward the institution of slavery were essentially similar. In Pennsylvania, as in Barbados, most Quakers saw no contradiction between Christianity and bondage; they saw no contradiction between one Christian holding another Christian in bondage. If they felt pressed to offer some justification for their stance, then that could be provided by their interpretation of the Scriptures. Africans were brought to Pennsylvania during the 1680s and 1690s, initially from other parts of English America, as a result of the trading links established so very rapidly between Philadelphia and the outside world. Their numbers remained comparatively small, however, principally because William Penn was so very successful in attracting British and continental European migrants to his colony. The offer of generous land grants, religious freedom, and what by the standards of the time was a humane criminal code all acted as a magnet to attract a flood of settlers not only from Europe but from other parts of English America.

William Penn chose not to outlaw the institution of slavery in Pennsylvania, and through the 1680s and 1690s the African component of the colony began to grow, but it did so in the context of small-scale slavery broadly comparable to that of New York and the New England colonies. As in these other northern colonies, enslaved Africans were employed in every sector of Pennsylvania's rapidly growing economy but were never of fundamental importance to the functioning of that economy. By the early eighteenth century there were still only around 1,300 people of African descent in Pennsylvania, and they accounted for just over 7 percent of the colony's population.

By no means all of the Quakers who settled in Pennsylvania chose to invest in enslaved African workers, but the vast majority of those who did kept whatever doubts and uncertainties they may have had to themselves. On the surface, at any rate, they were untroubled by the fact of their slaveholding. Consciences could be eased, if not entirely satisfied, by following at least a part of George Fox's instructions: seeing to it that their slaves received regular religious instruction. Most chose to ignore Fox's insistence that slavery ought not to be a permanent status imposed upon Africans. However, there were in the Pennsylvania of the 1690s a few Quakers who did take heed of Fox's strictures, who tried to force the Quaker majority to confront the issue of slaveholding and slave trading.

In 1696 a group of Rhineland Quakers who had settled at Germantown raised the question of the legitimacy of slaveholding with the Philadelphia Monthly Meeting. That Meeting found it impossible to come up with an easy answer and chose to shelve the matter for consideration at some future point. In the meantime, Quakers continued to hold enslaved Africans, and some had absolutely no misgivings about making money from the transatlantic slave trade. As of 1700 there was as little evidence of a significant body of antislavery thought in Pennsylvania as there was in any of the other English American colonies. It would not be until the middle years of the eighteenth century, largely through the efforts of John Woolman and Anthony Benezet, that opposition to slavery and the slave trade would begin to emerge as an accepted part of mainstream Quaker thought on both sides of the Atlantic.

The English had begun their colonization of the New World in the late sixteenth century, at Roanoke, without intending to enslave anyone. By the end of the following century, in environments as different as New England and the Chesapeake, Barbados and Pennsylvania, the enslavement of people of West African descent had become an integral, deeply entrenched, and largely uncontested fact of life everywhere in English America. It was not by the original design of the English, and neither was it purely by chance, that "Negro" and "Slave" had "grown Homogeneous and Convertible." As the eighteenth century dawned, there was no reason to believe that this situation would change in the foreseeable future.

Suggestions for
Further Reading

Chapter 1

David Brion Davis's monumental study *The Problem of Slavery in Western Culture* (Ithaca, N.Y.: Cornell University Press, 1967) remains by far and away the most comprehensive analysis of the content and evolution of European discourses on slavery prior to the mid-eighteenth century. Two works that provide an excellent survey of the social makeup of late sixteenth- and seventeenth-century England are Keith Wrightson's *English Society, 1580–1680* (London: Hutchinson, 1982) and J. A. Sharpe's *Early Modern England: A Social History, 1550–1760* (London: Edward Arnold, 1987). Ann Kussmaul provides more detail about the character and extent of servitude in her *Servants in Husbandry in Early Modern England* (Cambridge, Eng.: Cambridge University Press, 1981). R. J. Steinfeld adopts a longer-term view of English labor law in his *The Invention of Free Labor: The Employment Relation in English Law and Culture, 1350–1870* (Chapel Hill, N.C.: University of North Carolina Press, 1991). Paul Slack's "Vagrants and Vagrancy in England, 1598–1644," *The English Historical Review*, 27

(1974): 360–79, provides some useful insights into the mobility of ordinary English people and the ways in which the governing classes sought to deal with it. It was this mobility that ultimately produced so many indentured servants for England's plantation colonies. The social and geographic origins of these seventeenth-century migrants have prompted a sharp debate among historians. Important contributions to this debate include Mildred Campbell, "Social Origins of Some Early Americans," in J. M. Smith, ed., *Seventeenth-Century America* (Chapel Hill, N.C.: University of North Carolina Press, 1959); David Souden, "Rogues, Whores, and Vagabonds?: Indentured Servant Immigrants to North America and the Case of Mid-Seventeenth Century Bristol," *Social History*, I, no. 3 (1978): 23–41; David Galenson, "The Social Origins of Some Early Americans," *The William and Mary Quarterly*, Third Ser., XXXVI (1979): 264–87; and Galenson, " 'Middling People or Common Sort'? The Social Origins of Some Early Americans Re-examined," with a rebuttal by Mildred Campbell, *The William and Mary Quarterly*, Third Ser., XXXVI (1979): 499–541.

Chapter 2

There is a substantial body of literature that deals with the overseas expansion of England that got under way in the sixteenth century. Particularly important contributions include K. R. Andrews, Nicholas P. Canny, and P. E. H. Hair, eds., *The Westward Enterprise: English Activities in Ireland, the Atlantic, and America, 1480–1650* (Liverpool, Eng.: Liverpool University Press, 1979); K. R. Andrews, *Trade, Plunder, and Settlement: Maritime Enterprise and the Genesis of the British Empire, 1480–1630* (Cambridge, Eng.: Cambridge University Press, 1984); and D. B. Quinn, *Explorers and Colonies: Amer-*

ica, 1500–1625 (London: Hambledon, 1990). There are several studies that deal specifically with Anglo-Irish relations in the sixteenth century. An older but still useful work is D. B. Quinn's *The Elizabethans and the Irish* (Ithaca, N.Y.: Cornell University Press, 1966). The significance of England's activities in Ireland for the English colonization of the New World is dealt with by Nicholas P. Canny in "The Ideology of English Colonization: From Ireland to America," *The William and Mary Quarterly*, Third Ser., XXX (1973): 575–98, and in *Kingdom and Colony: Ireland in the Atlantic World, 1500–1800* (Baltimore: Johns Hopkins University Press, 1988). For contemporary accounts of the earliest English voyages to the Americas, and descriptions of the peoples encountered there, see Richard Hakluyt, *The Principal Navigations, Voyages, Traffiques, and Discoveries of the English Nation* (London: G. Bishop, R. Newberie, and R. Barker, 1598–1600; new edition, New York: Viking Press, 1965), and Samuel Purchas, *Hakluytus Posthumus or Purchas His Pilgrimes, Contayning a History of the World in Sea Voyages and Lande Travells by Englishmen and Others* [1625], 20 vols. (Glasgow: J. MacLehose and Sons, 1905–07). John White's sketches form the subject matter of Paul Hulton's *America 1585: The Complete Drawings of John White* (Chapel Hill, N.C.: University of North Carolina Press, 1984). The cultural frontiers between the English and the other peoples they encountered both in the Old World and in the New are the subject matter of *Strangers Within the Realm: The Cultural Margins of the First British Empire* (Chapel Hill, N.C.: University of North Carolina Press, 1991), edited by Bernard Bailyn and Philip D. Morgan. The essays in this collection emphasize that these boundaries were not static and that they involved cultural interaction rather than simply the successful imposition of a dominant English culture.

These themes are also pursued by Urs Bitterli in his *Cultures in Conflict: Encounters Between European and Non-European Cultures, 1492–1800* (Cambridge, Eng.: Polity Press, 1989). Generally speaking, historians have dealt separately with the initial encounters between the English, indigenous Americans, and West Africans. There is a vast scholarship on the forging of sixteenth- and early-seventeenth-century English impressions, and expectations, of native Americans. Important studies include W. R. Jacobs, *Dispossessing the American Indian* (Norman, Okla.: University of Oklahoma Press, 1972); Francis Jennings, *The Invasion of America: Indians, Colonialism, and the Cant of Conquest* (Chapel Hill, N.C.: University of North Carolina Press, 1975); H. C. Porter, *The Inconstant Savage: England and the North American Indians, 1500–1600* (London: Duckworth, 1979); Bernard Sheehan, *Savagism and Civility: Indians and Englishmen in Colonial Virginia* (Cambridge, Eng.: Cambridge University Press, 1980); James Axtell, *The Invasion Within: The Contest of Cultures in Colonial North America* (New York and Oxford, Eng.: Oxford University Press, 1985); Axtell, *After Columbus: Essays in the Ethnohistory of Colonial North America* (New York: Oxford University Press, 1989); and Karen O. Kupperman, *Settling with the Indians: The Meeting of English and Indian Cultures in America, 1580–1640* (London: Dent, 1980). Kupperman provides a detailed analysis of the encounters at Roanoke in her *Roanoke: The Abandoned Colony* (Totowa, N.J.: Rowman and Allenheld, 1984). For a collection of contemporary English and continental European accounts of West Africa, see John W. Blake, ed., *Europeans in West Africa, 1450–1560*, 2 vols. (London: The Hakluyt Society, 1942). The standard text on the initial formulation of English impressions of West Africans remains Winthrop D. Jordan's *White over Black: American Attitudes*

Toward the Negro, 1550–1812 (Chapel Hill, N.C.: University of North Carolina Press, 1966). Valuable insights into the West African component of the Early Modern English population are provided by F. O. Shyllon in his *Black People in Britain, 1555–1833* (London: Oxford University Press for the Institute of Race Relations, 1977) and in two works by James Walvin, *The Black Presence: A Documentary History of the Negro in England* (London: Orbach & Chambers, 1971) and *Black and White: The Negro and English Society, 1555–1945* (London: Allen Lane The Penguin Press, 1973). For the beginnings and early history of the transatlantic slave trade, see John K. Thornton, *Africa and Africans in the Making of the Atlantic World, 1400–1680* (Cambridge, Eng.: Cambridge University Press, 1992). For estimates of the number of people forcibly removed from West Africa during the duration of the slave trade, see Philip D. Curtin, *The Atlantic Slave Trade: A Census* (Madison, Wis.: University of Wisconsin Press, 1969).

Chapter 3

For comprehensive surveys of the English attempt to establish themselves in the Caribbean, see C. Bridenbaugh and R. Bridenbaugh, *No Peace Beyond the Line* (New York: Oxford University Press, 1972); Richard Sheridan, *Sugar and Slavery: An Economic History of the British West Indies, 1623–1775* (Eagle Hall, Barbados: Caribbean Universities Press, 1974); and Richard S. Dunn, *Sugar and Slaves: The Rise of the Planter Class in the English West Indies, 1624–1712* (Chapel Hill, N.C.: University of North Carolina Press, 1972). What proved to be the short-lived English settlement on Providence Island is dealt with by Karen O. Kupperman in her *Providence Island, 1630–1641: The Other Puritan Colony* (Cambridge, Eng.: Cambridge

University Press, 1993). For two recent studies that focus specifically on Barbados, see G. A. Puckrein, *Little England: Plantation Society and Anglo-Barbadian Politics, 1627–1800* (New York: New York University Press, 1984), and Hilary McD. Beckles, *White Servitude and Black Slavery in Barbados, 1627–1715* (Knoxville, Tenn.: University of Tennessee Press, 1989). For contemporary accounts of Barbados, see Richard Ligon, *A True and Exact History of the Island of Barbados* (London, 1657; rpt. Frank Cass & Co. Ltd., 1970) and "Extracts from Henry Whistler's Journal of the West India Expedition," in C. H. Firth, ed., *The Narrative of General Venables, with an Appendix of Papers Relating to the Expedition to the West Indies and the Conquest of Jamaica, 1654–1655* (London: Camden Society Publications, 1900). For a comprehensive account of the English acquisition of Jamaica, see S. A. G. Taylor, *The Western Design: An Account of Cromwell's Expedition to the Caribbean* (Kingston, Jamaica: Institute of Jamaica, 1969). The definitive study of the origins and early history of slavery in South Carolina remains Peter H. Wood's *Black Majority: Negroes in Colonial South Carolina from 1670 Through the Stono Rebellion* (New York: Knopf, 1974). Wood emphasizes the Barbadian connection, as does Richard S. Dunn in his "The English Sugar Islands and the Founding of South Carolina," in T. H. Breen, ed., *Shaping Southern Society: The Colonial Experience* (New York: Oxford University Press, 1976).

Chapter 4

There is a substantial scholarly literature on the founding and early history of Virginia. For the opinions and experiences of one of the leading participants in the settlement of what proved to be England's first mainland American colony, see Philip L.

Barbour, ed., *The Complete Works of Captain John Smith*, 3 vols. (Chapel Hill, N.C.: University of North Carolina Press, 1986). Several recent works deal with the supply of indentured servants to the Chesapeake colonies, their conditions of work, and their postindenture opportunities. These issues are dealt with at length by Edmund S. Morgan in his *American Slavery—American Freedom: The Ordeal of Colonial Virginia* (New York: W. W. Norton, 1975). A view similar to Morgan's— that changing demographic and economic circumstances assumed a greater importance than race and ethnicity in determining the precise timing of the transition to racial slavery in different parts of English America—is presented by R. Bean and R. Thomas in their "The Adoption of Slave Labour in British America," in H. A. Gemery and J. S. Hogendorn, eds., *The Uncommon Market: Essays in the Economic History of the Atlantic Slave Trade* (New York: Academic Press, 1979), and by D. W. Galenson in his *Traders, Planters and Slaves: Market Behavior in Early America* (Cambridge, Eng., and New York: Cambridge University Press, 1980) and *White Servitude in Colonial America: An Economic Analysis* (Cambridge, Eng., and New York: Cambridge University Press, 1981). Works that deal specifically with indentured servants include Russell R. Menard's "From Servant to Freeholder: Status, Mobility, and Property in Seventeenth-Century Maryland," *The William and Mary Quarterly*, Third Ser., XXX (1973): 347–64, and James Horn's *Adapting to a New World: English Society in the Seventeenth-Century Chesapeake* (Chapel Hill, N.C.: University of North Carolina Press, 1995). Scholars have disagreed about the precise status and treatment accorded Virginia's comparatively small West African population prior to the mid-seventeenth century. These themes are dealt with by Jordan in *White over Black* and by T. H. Breen and Stephen Innes in their *Myne Owne Ground: Race and Freedom on Virginia's Eastern Shore, 1640–1676* (New York: Oxford University Press, 1980). Although concerned primarily with the eighteenth century, Allan Kulikoff's *Tobacco and Slaves: The Development of Southern Cultures in the Chesapeake, 1680–1800* (Chapel Hill, N.C.: University of North Carolina Press, 1986) includes a valuable discussion of the transition from indentured to involuntary servitude. The late seventeenth century is also the focus of Russell R. Menard's "From Servant to Slave: The Transformation of the Chesapeake's Labor System," *Southern Studies*, XVI (1977): 355–90.

Chapter 5

For Puritan impressions of, and their relations with, indigenous Americans, see Alden T. Vaughan, *New England Frontier: Puritans and Indians, 1620–1675* (Boston: Little, Brown, 1965), and Neal Salisbury, *Manitou and Providence: Indians, Europeans and the Making of New England* (New York and Oxford, Eng.: Oxford University Press, 1982). There is an abundant literature on the social, ethnic, and religious ideology that informed the Puritans' views on freedom and bondage. The most relevant recent studies include T. H. Breen, *Puritans and Adventurers* (New York: Oxford University Press, 1980); V. D. Anderson, *New England's Generation: The Great Migration and the Formation of Society and Culture in the Seventeenth Century* (Cambridge, Eng.: Cambridge University Press, 1991); Stephen Innes, *The Long Argument: English Puritanism and the Shaping of New England Culture* (Chapel Hill, N.C.: University of North Carolina Press, 1991); and Innes, *Creating the Commonwealth: The Economic Culture of Puritan New England* (New York and London: W. W. Norton, 1994). For the laws of freedom and bondage devised by the Puritans, see Max Farrand, ed., *The Laws and Liberties of Massachusetts* (Cambridge, Mass.: Harvard University Press, 1929). Scholars have paid scant attention to the enslavement of West Africans in seventeenth-century New England. L. J. Greene, *The Negro in Colonial New England, 1628–1776* (New York: Columbia University Press, 1942) remains the only book-length study of the colonial period, while R. C. Twombly and R. H. Moore, "Black Puritan: The Negro in Seventeenth-Century New England," *The William and Mary Quarterly*, Third Ser., XXIV (1967): 224–42, provide a short but informative survey of the seventeenth century. For Cotton Mather's views on enslaved Africans, see his *The Negro Christianized: An Essay to Excite and Assist That Good Work, the Instruction of Negro-Servants in Christianity* (Boston: B. Green, 1706). For the debate between Sewall and Saffin, see Samuel Sewall, *The Selling of Joseph* (Boston; 1700; rpt. New York: Arno Press, 1969), and John Saffin, *A Brief and Candid Answer to a Late Printed Sheet, Entitled, the Selling of Joseph* (Boston: n.p., 1701). The beginnings and early history of racial slavery in Pennsylvania have been largely ignored by scholars. For an important exception see Gary B. Nash, "Slaves and Slaveowners in Colonial Philadelphia," *The William and Mary Quarterly*, Third Ser., XXX (1973): 223–56. George Fox's views on bondage, and the duties of Christian masters toward their servants and slaves, are to be found in his *Gospel Family-Order, Being a Short Discourse Concerning the Ordering of Families, Both of Whites, Blacks and Indians* (London: n.p., 1676). Comparatively little has been written about racial slavery in late seventeenth-century New York. The standard work remains Edgar J. McManus, *A History of Negro Slavery in New York* (Syracuse, N.Y.: Syracuse University Press, 1970).

Index